The Ants Are My Friends

The Ants Are My Friends

A PUNDERFUL CELEBRATION OF SONG

RICHARD LEDERER and STAN KEGEL

Marion Street Press, Inc.
www.marionstreetpress.com
Oak Park, Illinois

ISBN 978-1-933338-22-4
Printed in U.S.A.

Marion Street Press, Inc.
PO Box 2249
Oak Park, IL 60303
866-443-7987
www.marionstreetpress.com

To Debbie, Ken, Jeff, and Robbie for all the joy
they have given me over the years
and to the memory of Audrey Kegel
— *Stan Kegel*

To my nephews and nieces – and to Kathy Lowe,
who writes the music of the heart
– *Richard Lederer*

Contents

Forewordplay

An ancient jungle king tyrannized his subjects and forced them to build him one elaborate throne after another – first of mud, then bamboo, then tin, then copper, and so on. When the king became tired of each royal chair, he would store it in the attic of his grass hut. One day the attic collapsed under the weight of the items stored in it, and the royal chairs came crashing down on the chief's head and killed him.

The moral of the tale: *People who live in grass houses shouldn't stow thrones.*

You've just been the victim of a set-up pun, a conspiracy of narrative and wordplay. In set-up punnery, the punster contrives an imaginary situation that leads up to a climax cunningly and punningly based upon a well-known sequence of words. The *pun*ch line may consist of an expression of a literary line (*the koala tea of Mercy is not strained*), a biblical passage (*many are cold, but few are frozen),* a title (*boyfoot bear with teak of Chan*), a movie line *(I wouldn't send a knight out on a dog like this),* a law *(transporting gulls across staid lions),* a slogan *(we will tell no whine before its time),* or, as in the set-up pun that began this disquisition, a well-known expression — here a punny version of *people who live* *in glass houses shouldn't throw stones.*

But the sprightliest and most popular of these set-up puns (also called groaners) reach a foreordained conclusion that consists of a line or lines from a popular song. These are among the most punderful specimens of wordplay because songs are the sound tracks of our lives. *Pun*ch lines that include lyrics provide instant recognition of the words being punned, creating a doubly satisfying response. And with that recognition, we hope that you, dear reader, will find yourself singing the more than 200 *pun*ch lines that bounce through this book and in your head, as part of a treasured memory.

Here are some of those lines without their set-up narratives.

The ants are my friends

Chess nuts boasting by an open foyer

I've thrown a custard in her face.

The yellow rows of taxis

I'd love to be an Oscar winner, Meyer.

Oh, dutiful, voracious spies

We suspect that each of these lyrical lines sets off a melody singing in your thoughts — sort of like *dee-jay vu*. You know how it works: The song is over, but the malady lingers on.

We think you'll enjoy seeing if you figured out the original lyrics that inspired each *pun*ch line. If you wish to check the lyrics in the form they existed before their creative makeovers, have a look at "The Answers, My Friends" at the end of each chapter. You'll also find out who wrote the music and words to each song.

We don't want to blow our own horns, but we are feeling fit as fiddles, and we don't fiddle around or play second fiddle to anyone. We don't wish to harp on this subject, and we'll never play it by ear and give you a second-string performance. We won't ever soft-pedal any aspect of the musical punnery, and we'll always pull out all the stops. We, your unsung heroes, will never offer you too much sax and violins. Rather, we wish simply to drum up enthusiasm for melodic wordplay that's right up your Tin Pan Alley.

We may not know our brass from our oboe, but there's one thing we know for sure: It's time to face the music.

Richard Lederer, San Diego, California
Stan Kegel, Orange, California

Chapter 1

Face the Music

Being Unshellfish

Larry Lobster and Sam Clam were best friends. They did everything together. The only difference between them was that Larry was the nicest lobster ever, and Sam, well let's just say he was not so virtuous. Larry and Sam did so much together that they even died together. Larry went to heaven and Sam went to hell.

One day Saint Peter came up to Larry and said, "Larry, you know you are the nicest lobster we ever had up here. Everyone likes you, but you seem to be a bit depressed. Tell me what's bothering you. Maybe I can help."

Larry replied, "Well, don't get me wrong, Pete. I like it up here and everything, but I really miss my good friend Sam Clam. We used to do everything

The Ants Are My Friends

together."

Saint Peter pitied Larry and said, "I tell you what. I can arrange it so that you can go down to hell tomorrow and visit Sam for twenty-four hours. How does that sound?" This made Larry very happy. He rose bright and early the next morning and grabbed his wings, his harp, and his halo and got on the elevator to hell.

When the doors opened, he was met by Sam. They hugged each other and off they went. You see, in hell Sam owned a disco. They spent the day there together and had a great time. At the end of the day, Larry and Sam said their good-byes, and up Larry elevated. When he stepped off the elevator, he was greeted by Saint Peter, who blocked the doorway to Heaven. "Larry Lobster," Saint Peter asked, "Didn't you forget something?"

Larry looked around and said, "No, I don't think so. I have my halo and my wings."

"Yes, but what about your harp?"

Larry gasped and said, "Oh dear, *I left my harp in Sam Clam's disco!*"

What's Yours is Mayan

Many anthropologists and historical mathematicians claimed that the ancient Mayans figured out the ratio of a circle's circumference to its diameter to an exactitude unknown until modern times.

But Herr Professor Doktor Fliegelberger's reputation was made when he conclusively showed that claim to be fraudulent. Fliegelberger offered his iron-clad thesis in his groundbreaking article, *"Bye, Bye, Mesoamerican Pi."*

Elvis Lives

Andrew's mother gave him ten dollars to buy lunch for himself and his sister Terri at the diner down the street. On the way, they passed a man selling puppies for ten dollars each. Unable to resist, Andrew bought one, named it Elvis, and went home.

While he stayed outside, playing with it, Terri went inside. "Back so soon?" her mother asked.

"Yes," said Terri. "I'm afraid we never made it to the diner."

"Why not?"

"Because Andrew spent ten dollars on Elvis."

"Elvis?"

"That's right," explained Terri. *"He ate nothin', bought a hound dog."*

What a Drag

By day he's an Elvis pretender,
But moonlights as Cher 'cuz he's slender.
   Disillusioned, I guess,
   He's now hung up his dress
And sings, *"I'm returning to gender."*

Gaining Leverage

"Give me a lever long enough and a prop strong enough," wrote the inventor and mathematician Archimedes, "and I can single-handedly move the world." In fact, Archimedes came up with all sorts of uses for the lever. He demonstrated how the lever could be used to lift heavy rocks, how the lever could be built into some musical instruments, and how the lever could be a powerful instrument of war.

Finally, he put all his ideas into a book and titled it *Fifty Ways to Love Your Lever.*

Say Cheese

All gourmets know about Holland's great cheeses: edam and gouda. Noted for their mild but unmistakable pungency, edam and gouda are enjoyed in Holland and throughout the world.

Most cheeses attract buyers through taste and odor, but the color of the cheese is also a vital factor. The most exquisite edams and goudas are dark, creamy yellow; the best are almost a creamy orange. In fact, most knowledgeable cheese experts prefer that orange color.

The leading Chinese cheese-making family in Holland was a family called Yung. The Yungs produced fine edam and gouda, but they could never get their goudas to develop the rich dark orange hue of the finest Dutch goudas. This hurt sales significantly.

It has always been against the Dutch cheese manufacturers' art to add artificial ingredients to genuine cheese. Nonetheless, the Yung family began adding artificial coloring to their cheese to create the most saleable appearance. In the Netherlands today, *only the Yung dye gouda.*

Gator Aid

When our local Chinese restaurant was booked for a large banquet, they decided to serve an exotic delicacy — crocodile meat. The chef devised a recipe involving stir-fried whole crocodile, accompanied by garlic, broccoli, and sweet red peppers. But when the time came to cook the concoction, the chef had a problem. He couldn't fit the *wok around the croc.*

A Stock Answer

Bernie's wife was cleaning the house like a mad woman when she asked him to run to the store and pick up another bottle of floor cleaner and a Sierra Mist. Bernie hustled over to the store and figured while he was there, he'd pick up a six-pack of Bud Ice for himself.

The store clerk explained that the three items Bernie wanted were sold out, explaining, "Sorry, *no more Mist or Ice, guy; no more Mr. Clean.*"

Right on the Nose

President Dwight Eisenhower's mother had a sister. This lady constantly had trouble in bright sunshine because her nose was so sensitive that the skin peeled off every summer.

Her doctor made a simple remedy, a small cone of paper (like a dunce cap), which she stuck onto her nose at the first sign of sun.

Do you believe this? I didn't until Mick Jagger sang about it. *"Ike's aunt gets nose hat. Is fact, son."*

Battle of the Bottles

A major soft drink manufacturer decided that providing choices in the container size in the six-packs of its beverages might help move the product off the shelves. The unique selling idea was to have several different container sizes in the very same six-pack.

One of the most successful packages comprised two 250 ml bottles, two 500 ml bottles, and two 1000 ml bottles. To the bottler's surprise, after purchasing the beverage, most people chose to drink from the 1000 ml container first. Postmarketing research showed why: It was *the liter of the pack.*

Hot dog!

Cyndi Lauper was having a cookout with her family and suggested to her daughter that she might like to help cook the hot dogs. Her daughter replied that she'd rather just split open and toast the bread over the fire. "You know, mom," the kid suggested. *"Grills just want two half buns."*

Going Nuts

Ol' Jedediah was out hunting for rabbits and squirrels. As he rounded a stand of trees, high up on one large limb sat the largest squirrel he'd ever seen. It must have weighed 100 pounds!

Taking careful aim with his trusty musket, Jed let loose a blast and felled that monster squirrel with one shot. Critters large and small gathered to watch Jed truss up his catch and drag it back to his cabin.

There was much rejoicing as the family greeted Jed with his huge trophy. They decided to have an outdoor feast and a couple of the children dragged out the large steel washtub and put it over the fire. Jed's wife slopped a bunch of oil in the makeshift frying pan and in went the monster.

Alas, try as they might, the darned thing just would not cook, no matter how hot they made the fire underneath.

While they were stoking the fire even hotter, they heard snickering in the trees close to the cabin. Up on one branch was a veritable chorus line of little squirrels, just laughing and dancing around. Jed asked what was so funny. They told him he'd never succeed in preparing his 100-pound squirrel in the makeshift frying pan.

When he asked why, with one voice the squirrels chimed: *"Big squirrels don't fry!"*

Not-So-Clearwater

Rock festival sign and insight:
Clearwater Revival tonight.
   Over and over,
   Be ye hipster or rover:
"There's a bathroom on the right!"

Pants on Fire

The play *Abie's Irish Rose* is about an Irish woman, Rose, who marries a Jewish man, Abie, despite their families' objections. In the story, an old boyfriend of Rose's shows up at their home demanding $10,000 that he claimed he lent to Rose. Rose and the audience know that the fellow's claim is a complete fabrication. Still, the former suitor insists on payment and grows increasingly belligerent. As the fellow's aggression escalates, Rose turns to her husband and pleads, *"Abie, won't you fight my liar?"*

A Ghost Graduate Course

A famous ghostbuster once spent a night in an old house reputedly haunted by the spirit of Sir John de Birmingham. According to his professional manual, he would have to hum a certain passage by Mozart, but under no circumstances leave it unfinished. If he failed to reach the end of the music, the wretched wraith would wreak terrible vengeance. Should he succeed in completing the passage, Sir John would leave him in peace.

All went well until the stroke of 3 a.m. Suddenly, the phantom appeared! Prepared for this, the ghostbuster began to hum quietly but precisely the passage, as he had practiced it. Nearing its end, he was relieved to note that Sir John's features were placid.

Suddenly, however, a second spirit appeared over Sir John's head! This caused our hero to lose his concentration and leave the passage unfinished. An unearthly snarl burst from the ethereal lips of Sir John, followed by a stream of curses. In terror, the ghostbuster fled the house.

Ever since, the man's colleagues in the profession have asked him, *"Did your shooing hum lose its quaver on the dead ghost over knight?"*

Cliffhanger

After finding Dr. Livingstone, Stanley and his wife decided to tour Africa and were captured by some unfriendly natives, tied together with a long piece of leather, and left dangling over a large cliff. That evening, the natives danced and chanted around the campfire, and as each member passed the leather strap holding the unfortunate couple, he gave it a whack with a stick, causing it to weaken a bit more. As the chanting grew louder and louder, Stanley looked at his wife romantically and said, "Listen, darling. *They're fraying our thong!"*

The Answers, My Friends

Being Unshellfish: "I left my heart in San Francisco" (*I Left My Heart in San Francisco* by George Cory and Douglas Cross)

What's Yours is Mayan: "Bye, bye, Miss American Pie" (*American Pie* by Don McLean)

Elvis Lives: "He ain't nothing but a hound dog" (*Hound Dog* by Mike Stoller and Jerry Leiber)

What a Drag: "Return to sender" (*Return to Sender* by Otis Blackwell and Winfield Scott)

Gaining Leverage: "Fifty ways to leave your lover" (*Fifty Ways to Leave Your Lover* by Paul Simon);

Say Cheese: "Only the good die young" (*Only the Good Die Young* by Billy Joel)

Gator Aid: "Rock around the clock" (*Rock around the Clock* by Max Freedman and Jimmy DeKnight)

A Stock Answer: "No more Mr. Nice Guy; no more Mr. Clean" (*No More Mr. Nice Guy* by Alice Cooper and Michael Bruce)

Right on the Nose: "I can't get no satisfaction" (*Satisfaction* by Keith Richards and Mick Jagger)

Battle of the Bottles: "The leader of the pack" (*Leader of the Pack* by Ellie Greenwich, Jeff Barry, and George "Shadow" Morton)

Hot dog!: "Girls just want to have fun" (*Girls Just Want to Have Fun* by Robert Hazard);

Going Nuts: "Big girls don't cry" (*Big Girls Don't Cry* by Bob Crewe and Bob Gaudio)

Not-So-Clearwater: "There's a bad moon on the rise" (*Bad Moon Rising* by J. Fogerty)

Pants on Fire: "Baby, won't you light my fire" (*Light My Fire* by Robbie Kreeger)

A Ghost Graduate Course: "Did your chewing gum lose its flavor on the bed post overnight?" (*Does Your Chewing Gum Lose Its Flavor on the Bedpost Overnight?* by Marty Bloom, Ernest Breuer, and Billy Rose)

Cliffhanger: "They're playing our song" (*They're Playing Our Song* by Marvin Hamlisch and Carole Bayer Sager)

Chapter 2

Love is All You Need

A Wonder-ful Woman

Lost in the mist of history is fact that that Wonder Woman once married tycoon Howard Hughes. But, alas, he was turned off by her alpha woman assertiveness, and she was horrified by his drug use. Seeking a new mate, the super heroine decided she wanted a more cerebral and settled husband. So she married Richard Nixon's Secretary of State, Henry Kissinger, whom she had met while fighting international criminals. She then informed all her super friends, *"I'm Wonder Hughes Kissinger now."*

The World Is My Oyster

A seafood restaurant was well known for its shellfish. Diners lavished extravagant praise on the restaurant's offerings, but the shellfish came in for particular accolades.

A few diners discovered the ultimate treat when eating oysters — perfectly shaped and valuable pearls. Yet even the amazing oyster cannot create a perfect pearl every time. One diner had a negative experience.

While enjoying his oysters one evening, he bit something hard. Unfortunately, upon removing the impediment from his mouth, he found it not to be a perfectly round, smooth pearl, but one with bumps, edges, and dirt on it. Having bitten into it, he sustained a broken tooth and required extensive dental surgery. His experience stayed with him for a long time, and his chronic discomfort caused him to realize that *a gritty pearl is like a malady.*

A Lot of Gaul

Slaves on the Nile used to shear the barnacles and fungus from the bottoms of the Arab dhows and sometimes the dhows would fall over and crush the poor devils. The slaves were guarded by mercenaries from Gaul, and the heat of the Middle East made them sleepy. The acid from the barnacles underneath the dhows irritated the skin quite a lot, and the only suitable balm available was highly perfumed lentils.

One day, an Arab dhow fell on top of the Gauls. The wretched men moaned as the acid burned through their leather trousers, and a foreman stood on a hill and sang this timeless lament: *"When sheared dhows fall over sleepy warden Gauls, I'm getting scented lentils over you."*

Nothing but the Tooth

An animal orthodontist who practiced in Iowa was called one day by a frantic farmer in Australia. "Help, sir!" he cried, "I just got braces for a hundred of my sheep, and the local sheep orthodontist just died! I need a responsible animal dentist to come care for my flock!"

The orthodontist was moved, and a good fee was offered, so he promptly flew to Australia for what he figured would be a week or two of work. But he found that he was entirely unfamiliar with the orthodontic equipment the sheep had been given, and he spent a whole six months in Australia trying to figure out the foreign braces. When he finally boarded a plane for home, he sighed with happiness. "At last, *I'll be seeing ewes in all the old familiar braces!*"

On the Lamb

In ancient times it was considered an honor to have one's daughter enter the Temple dedicated to Diana, the moon goddess. Once accepted, these daughters of Diana would pledge to remain chaste and serve their goddess forever.

Sophia was a dwarf. Although fully matured in her late teens, she was no more than three feet tall. Her loving parents, realizing that no man would likely want her for a wife, brought her to the Temple of Diana, where after extensive training, she became a maiden of Diana.

She was happy in her new life, until, on a visit to Athens, she saw a lad no taller than she was. They gravitated to each other and immediately fell head over sandals in love. Sophia could not bear to leave her new love and return to the temple, and the two fled to the Isle of Santorini to start a new life.

When Diana discovered the unfaithfulness of her maiden, she became enraged and searched until she found the loving couple. So angered was Diana that she immediately turned Sophia into a sheep. A poet seeing the events transpire wrote an ode telling the story of Sophia's love and Diana's revenge. It was known throughout Greece as *"Moon Mite Becomes Ewe."*

The Gain in Spain

Juan, a Spanish gentleman, fell in love with Carmencita, a most possessive girl. She had heard the gossip that his was a wandering eye, but it didn't surprise her because that trait was inherited from his primitive ancestors. Carmencita decided there was only one way she could be certain her man would remain faithful until she could exchange the alter for the halter.

By accompanying him everywhere, every waking moment, she became the village joke. But her vigilance was rewarded when she was able finally to wed her suitor without his ever once being unfaithful, a state of grace hitherto unheard of in all of Spain.

Everywhere she went, eager, inquiring maidens would ask her for the secret of her success. She unfailingly answered, *"You always herd the Juan you love."*

Mon Amy

Russ was leaving home for the Great Lakes Training Center to start his career in the Navy. His new wife, Amy, was filled with remorse and sadness. Russ was equally brokenhearted, but he felt that in these troubled times, he needed to serve his country. So he kissed his bride farewell and left for basic training.

Of course he took a framed portrait of Amy with him. Every night Russ would sit on his bunk, stare at the photo and long for his new wife. He would talk to himself and reminisce about their wonderful times together. Finally one of his bunkmates asked him what was going on. Russ just sighed and moaned, "I truly miss her, and that's why I *moon over my Amy."*

Tall, Dark, and Hairy

In the topical rain forests of Cameroon, Africa, there lived a band of western lowland gorillas. This band was isolated from other gorilla bands and was quite happy being a separate group and thereby not having to compete for food or space. However, a rather unique occurrence happened to this gorilla band.

It seemed that the mature females started giving birth to nothing but males! As the band matured, there was no way for the maturing males to procreate due to the lack of female gorillas to accommodate them.

So the band elders decided the oldest young male gorilla, Simba, would have to find a female western lowland gorilla outside the group to mate with.

The elders taught him how to find a mate and recognize the key characteristics for successfully breeding and raising offspring.

Once Simba had learned the ways of the older gorillas, he set out to find himself a mate. Day and night he trekked through the rain forests trying to find the ideal female gorilla. Even as he slept, he would fantasize about the mate he was seeking.

Finally, after months of searching, Simba came across another band of western lowland gorillas. He carefully watched them and was able to select a candidate that would suit his needs. Simba cautiously approached this lovely female and, in ape language, said to her, *"Gorilla my dreams, I love you."*

A Responsive Chord

Stevie Wonder played a gig in Tokyo, and the hall was packed to the rafters. Stevie asked for requests.

A little old Japanese man jumped out of his seat in the first row and shouted at the top of his voice, "Play a jazz chord! Play a jazz chord!"

Amazed that this guy knew about the jazz influences on Stevie's career, the blind impresario played an E minor scale and then segued into a difficult jazz melody.

When he finished the whole place went wild. The little old man jumped up again and shouted, "No, no, play a jazz chord, play a jazz chord."

A bit irritated by this, Stevie, being the professional that he is, dived straight into a jazz improvisation with his band around the B flat minor chord and again tore the place apart.

The crowd again went wild with this impromptu show of his technical expertise. The little old man jumped up again. "No, no! Play a jazz chord, play a jazz chord!"

Well, now truly irritated that this little guy didn't seem to appreciate his playing ability, Stevie said to him from the stage, "OK, mister, you get up here and do it!"

The little old man climbed up onto the stage, took hold of the mike, and sang, *"A jazz chord, to say I ruv you!"*

Monkee-ing Around

Mindy was upset.

Last week she'd gone to Pete's Restaurant for lunch. Sitting in the bar was this hunk. She made sure she ended up sitting next to him.

"Why the long face?" she'd asked.

He'd smiled a bit at the classic line, but his features quickly drew tight again.

"I think my wife's fooling around," he replied. "She's been, well, you know, different, when I get home the last few weeks."

He thumbed a small photo in his left hand. Mindy took a glance. This plain Jane wasn't worth getting upset about. She had the upper hand, and she knew it. She placed a few stray hairs to set off her eyes, adjusted her décolletage for maximum effect, and leaned closer.

It had been too easy. For a week now, they'd met every day at lunchtime. He'd be hers. Until today. He was there, but he wasn't there. Finally he spoke. "I won't be seeing you any more. My wife told me what was going on. She'd been going out, just like this, at lunchtime, looking for company. I guess I hadn't been there enough for her. She gave up on it and told me everything. So, thanks for listening. Bye." He dropped a twenty on the bar, drained his glass, and walked out.

So why shouldn't she be upset? *This daydream, he'd leave her for a crone coming clean.*

Fits Like a Glove

A smashing looking model was asked to pose for a glove ad. To heighten the effect of the product, she was asked to pose in the buff, wearing only the long, elegant gloves. As she sashayed out to the set, she thought, *"I'm in the nude for gloves."*

The Eyes of Taxes Are upon You

In the heyday of the Russian Empire, the representatives of monarchy were quite diligent in ferreting out any possible source of revenue. Naturally, the long-suffering peasantry used every mechanism to avoid the tax collectors, but sometimes circumstances conspired to defeat even the cleverest and most ambitious farmer.

The problem is well illustrated by the fate of one Ivan Sergeivitch, who invested a substantial sum of money in improving the fertility of his fields. As a result, his yields of barley, wheat, and other grains grew apace.

Soon he decided to turn his yield directly into consumer products, and he began selling a variety of baked goods, such as bread, rolls, and pastries. As his income increased, he invested in additional acreage, and in turn, in increased sales of his baked goods. In other words, he became the quintessential capitalist.

As sometimes happens, though, his productivity outstripped his ability to sell the finished product, and so he resorted to the inevitable: He put up signs along the roads advertising his bakery and its goods.

This unfortunate step brought him to the attention of the authorities, who imposed a list of punishing taxes on his once-thriving operation. As a neighbor pointed out to the once-again-poor Ivan, it was just another reason for the existence of the old Russian proverb: *"Don't let the tsars get in your ryes."*

The Answers, My Friend

The World Is My Oyster: "A pretty girl is like a melody" (*A Pretty Girl Is like a Melody* by Irving Berlin)

Nothing but the Tooth: "I'll be seeing you in all the old familiar places" (*I'll Be Seeing You* by Irving Kahal and Sammy Fain)

On the Lamb: "Moonlight becomes you" (*Moonlight Becomes You* by Johnny Burke and Jimmy Van Heusen)

The Gain in Spain: "You always hurt the one you love" (*You Always Hurt the One You Love* by Doris Fisher and Alan Roberts)

A Lot of Gaul: "I'm getting sentimental over you" (*I'm Getting Sentimental over You* by George Bassman and Ned Washington)

Mon Amy: "Moon over Miami" (*Moon over Miami* by Joe Burke and Edgar Leslie)

Tall, Dark, and Hairy: "Girl of my dreams, I love you" (*Girl of My Dreams* by Sunny Clapp)

A Responsive Chord: "I just called to say I love you" (*I Just Called to Say I Love You* by Stevie Wonder)

Monkee-ing Around: "This daydream, he'd leave her for a homecoming queen" (*Daydream Believer* by John Stewart)

Fits like a Glove: "I'm in the mood for love" (*I'm in the Mood for Love* by Jimmy McHugh and Dorothy Fields, from the film *Every Night at Eight)*

The Eyes of Taxes Are upon You: "Don't let the stars get in your eyes" (*Don't Let the Stars Get in Your Eyes* by Slim Willet)

Chapter 3

Golden Oldies

A Pun of Biblical Proportions

Have you seen the new musical comedy divinely inspired by The Ten Commandments? Its fun-filled biblical entertainment for the entire family includes the songs "I Took a Little Prophet from the Rushes on the Banks," "I was an Infant Basket Case," "I Talk to the Bush," "Your Wish is My Commandments," and "Take Two Tablets and Call Me in the Morning." Its most memorable hit song is "Runelight and Moses."

A Trunk-Aided Tail

During a coup attempt by a number of rebellious nobles, King George I had a huge mahogany rack constructed to punish the leaders of the uprising. His advisers transported the rack to the upcoming battle site, at a precipice overlooking the valley containing the enemy encampment, by renting forty pachyderms and hiring an African engineer with reputed expertise in harnessing the huge beasts for productive labor.

Unfortunately, shortly after their arrival at the scene, the elephants stampeded, carrying the ramp with the African on it tumbling down the hill, rolling over the opposition, and virtually destroying it. One of the survivors painfully cried out, "What in creation was that?"

An anguished companion stammered, "I'm not sure, but it looked like *a rambling rack from George's attack and an elephant engineer.*"

What's the Good Kurd?

Jalal was a vocal supporter of Kurdistan unification and the rights of his fellow countrymen living abroad. Because of his involvement in the politics of his country, Jalal had to travel a great deal. This upset his girlfriend, Shirien, who loved him deeply but found her feelings dampened by his frequent absences. While Jalal was away, Shirien fell in love with another man.

When Jalal returned from his travels, he found a note from Shirien, read it, and started wailing and tearing at his clothes.

"What's wrong?" asked one of his friends.

Another looked at the note and realized that the situation wasn't all that serious. The friend explained, *"He's only a Kurd in a jilted rage."*

Sam, Please Make the Pants Longer

One day a man and his wife got into a terrible fight. She became so angry that she shredded the legs of his favorite pair of pants. When he saw what she had done, he nearly broke down in tears because of how much those pants meant to him.

He took them to tailors near and far in an attempt to get them fixed as good as new, but not one would even attempt it. One day he finally found an old tailor who said he would try. "I have developed a new technique to reweave the fabric together so you will not be able to tell the pants had ever been damaged," bragged the old tailor. "It will be as if they are growing back together into a new pair of pants."

"That's perfect!" cried the man.

"It will take a long time, for it is a very involved process. It will also be expensive, but I am the only one in the world who can do this."

"Money is no object," stated the man, so the tailor began to fix his pants.

The man checked in every week to see how his pants were progressing, and every week the tailor showed him how the pants were growing slowly but steadily longer.

One day when the pants were at about mid-thigh the man walked into the shop, but all the shades were drawn and there was an atmosphere of mourning in the air.

An apprentice, recognizing the man from his frequent visits, explained that the tailor had died of a heart attack in his sleep the night before.

"I hate to ask," said the man, "at such a somber moment, but I'd like to know one thing. The pants he was working on for me, will they ever be finished?"

The apprentice looked at him sadly, finally shaking his bowed head. "I'm sorry, but *they stopped, shorts, never to grow again when the old man died.*"

Mend Your Ways

A tailor thought it fitting to take his young son into his very suitable business. Tailor, Jr. didn't think very much of the idea, but what father wants, father often gets.

Junior learned the trade. He understood the material things — the choice of fabric, the cutting, the fitting. All in all, he measured up quite well.

But try as he might, he could not master sewing. Whenever he tried his hand at it, his father scolded him that it was improperly done. "Undo it and try again."

Lots of thread was wasted — so much so that Sr. tried a new tack, applying kind words instead of harsh ones, alas, to no avail. One day in frustration, the father shouted, *"Spools rush in where wise mends fear to thread!"*

Net and Yahoo

Former Israeli Prime Minister Benjamin Netanyahu goes by the nickname "Bibi." His wife, in contrast to most Israeli "first ladies," took a more activist role in her country's affairs. At the first summit conference held between Israel and the PLO, Mrs. Netanyahu introduced her husband to PLO leader Arafat by saying, *"Yasir, that's my Bibi."*

Pi in the Sky

In Northern Germany there is an ancient village populated mainly by mathematicians. Now, these are not your ordinary run-of-the-mill quantum mechanical explorers or such. Rather they are trigonometric specialists. In fact, there are village holidays celebrating some of the more common trig functions, including one dealing with the side opposite over the side closest.

But that's going off on a tangent. The occasion at hand is this evening's bash, which celebrates the function relating the side opposite the hypotenuse. There will be bonfires and fireworks, and the pig is already in the ground. Yes, *there'll be a hot sine in the old town, tonight.*

It's About Time

Once upon a time, Alexander the Great was just Alexander, a mediocre, run-of-the-mill general. He tried hard, but usually arrived at the battle scene too early or too late, since watches and clocks hadn't yet been invented.

Alexander appeared doomed to obscurity, until a bright Macedonian lad, one Herbie, made a suggestion that changed history. "Sire," he said timidly, "I have been puttering about with diverse rare earths and chemical substances. I have not yet uncovered the secret of transforming base metals into gold, but I have discovered some phenomena that might be of use in our military endeavors."

"A new weapon?"

"No, sire. A simple device that will enable your eminence to accurately ascertain the proper moment for our armies to arrive upon the scene. It will work quite well until the Timex is invented."

"Very interesting. Tell me more."

"Well, you take this scrap of cloth, dip it into this

special liquid dye, and tie it around your wrist. As we march along in the heat of the day, the liquid gradually evaporates, causing the cloth to slowly change color at a highly predictable rate, providing an accurate gauge of how many hours have passed."

Alexander adopted the idea (taking full credit) and went on to greatness and immortality. And the invention that made it all possible? The piece of cloth that changed the world? It has henceforth been referred to as *Alexander's rag time-band*.

A Rare Medium Well Done

A butcher in New York had a flourishing business next to an exclusive apartment building in which many United Nations representatives lived. One of the representatives was a mysterious holy man from India who constantly berated the butcher for selling beef. Cattle, of course, was sacred in this mystic's Hindu religion. One day, the mystic became quite ill with severe anemia.

The doctor, after examining him, prescribed some meat for his diet; in fact, he suggested that beef liver might be the best diet supplement for him. This would supply both the iron and the Vitamin B-12 that were so deficient in his cultural diet.

The mystic reluctantly agreed that his health was too important to jeopardize. He went to the butcher to order some. The butcher, realizing that this was his chance to get back at the Indian for all his insults, decided to overcharge him by lying to him about the weight of the meat. He told his assistant, "When you put the meat on the scale, press down with your thumb on the scale in order to *weigh down upon the Swami's liver.*"

A Jewel of a Pun

There once was a mother whose daughter kept trying to elope with her intended. Always, however, in the nick of time, the mother caught them. After about twenty attempts, the daughter began to get desperate, when by chance, she read about an animal activist who painted bulls to camouflage them so they could escape from their owners. Alas, when the daughter asked the activist to similarly help her, he told her, *"I stain bulls, not constant elopers."*

Getting Oriented

I was planning to surprise my wife with a romantic Japanese dinner on Valentine's Day. I know all about teriyaki, gyoza, sashimi, and sake, and, let me tell you: *"If you knew sushi like I know sushi."*

I also knew that there's nothing like a fine wine to wake up a dish of sushi. You just have to make sure your wine isn't one of those artificial ones made from honey. *They call mead the grape pretender.*

Well, I guess if the waiter served my wife a fake wine for the dinner, she might end up singing, *"My phony valentine."*

A Mine is a Terrible Thing

Did you hear about the mining company executive who was famous for personally going down into the mines to settle labor differences? He took great relish in that part of his job and often was heard singing on the elevator as it lowered him down through the strata of rock, *"Gonna take a sedimental journey, gonna set my mine at ease."*

A Sonnet

An Indian chief with chronic stomach aches
goes to the tribe's medicine man to check
his health and get a cure. The shaman takes
an elk-hide thong he had around his neck
and gives it to the chief. "Each day you'll chew
a bite off this, grind it to bits and swallow,
and in a moon you should be good as new
provided that you take good care to follow
what I've prescribed." A month from then the chief
returns, but with the same old stomach pains.
He's eaten the whole thing, and to his grief
he is no better, bitterly complains,
"Everything that you told me, I have done.
The thong is ended, but the malady lingers on."

The Frown Princess

Oh, what a sad doll was Doleful Dorothy! She was
frowning when she woke each morning, and she was
crying when she retired each night. Hers was such a
continually somber life that one of her friends described her as "another-day-another-doleur."

She attracted so much attention in town, a song-
writer decided that Dottie's sad story might be written into a best-selling soul-wrenching ballad. He
labored long, and when he finished, he tried it on his
wife.

"Great," she exclaimed. "You'll have people sob-
bing in every night spot. What are you going to call
it?"

Said the tunesmith, "How about *'Mighty Lachry-
mose'?*"

Blimey! Slimy!

England recently was afflicted with a terrible plague of toads. They were hopping everywhere, jumping out of storm sewers, thronging the streets. It was amazing — truly *a froggy day in London town.*

Bag Lady

A rather harried and frazzled woman arrived at an airport one day struggling with a dilapidated old suitcase made entirely of Styrofoam. It was barely in one piece and covered with duct tape.

Seeing this, a security guard went over to help the poor lady with her things. As they walked to her gate, he inquired casually, "Madam, if I may ask, why are you carrying your things in this horrible old Styrofoam suitcase?"

She looked at him and kinda smiled as she replied, *"Even though it may crumble, there's no case like foam."*

San Simian

An African tribe, mostly swineherds and fishermen, lived on the shores of a bay. The bay had treacherous currents and water turgid with sand, but fishing was good and the tribe prospered. They attributed this to their sacrifices — a prize boar each year to every tribal god except the sea god, who got a gorilla. (A wise chieftain a few generations back had substituted gorilla sacrifice for human.)

One year, the tribesmen could not capture a gorilla. The chieftain asked the tribal wise-woman, the surviving member of a Swedish explorer couple who had lived with the tribe for many happy years, if they should substitute their best boar for the gorilla.

She was strongly against it, even to the point of suggesting herself as a human sacrifice. He was horrified and reminded her that porcine offerings had always pleased the other gods.

The time of sacrifice arrived. With prayers for the sea god's mercy, the shamans went through the usual rituals with the boar instead of the gorilla, culminating in its being taken to the middle of the bay and having its throat cut as it was thrown in.

Nothing went wrong and the next year was as prosperous as usual. After that, pigs replaced gorillas.

Moral: *Let a swine be your gorilla in a grainy, grainy bay. If your Swede decries, just tell her that a swine will always pay.*

Run of the Mill

In California, where the ground can resemble Jell-O, a temblor hit, and everybody in an office supply store took cover.

The packages of paper quivered like leaves — all

but one, which was wedged in so tightly that it, and it alone, didn't shake. Thinking it looked like a safe place to be, employee Donnie took shelter beside it, ducking to avoid the falling plaster. When the quake was over, and the store manager started counting heads, he asked, "Where's Donnie?" To which one of the other employees replied, *"Down by the old still ream."*

The Answers, My Friends

A Pun of Biblical Proportions: "Moonlight and roses" (*Moonlight and Roses,* adapted from *Andantino in D Flat* by Edwin H. Lemare)

A Trunk-Aided Tail: "I'm a Rambling wreck from Georgia Tech and a hell of an engineer" (*I'm a Rambling Wreck from Georgia Tech,* college fight song)

What's the Good Kurd?: "Only a bird in a gilded cage" (*Only a Bird in a Gilded Cage* by Harry Von Tilzer and Arthur A. Lamb)

Sam, Please Make the Pants Longer: "It stopped short, never to go again, when the old man died." (*My Grandfather's Clock* by Henry Clay Work)

Mend Your Ways: "Fools rush in where angels fear to tread" (*Fools Rush In* by Rube Bloom and Johnny Mercer)

Net and Yahoo: "Yes sir, that's my baby" (*Yes Sir, That's My Baby* by Walter Donaldson and Gus Kahn)

Pi in the Sky: "There'll be a hot time in the old town tonight" (*Hot Time in the Old Town* by Theodore Metz and Joe Hayden)

It's about Time: "Alexander's ragtime band"

(*Alexander's Ragtime Band* by Irving Berlin)

A Rare Medium Well Done: "Way down upon the Swanee River" (*Old Folks at Home* by Stephen Foster and E.P. Christy)

A Jewel of a Pun: "Istanbul, not Constantinople" (*Istanbul, Not Constantinople* by Nat Simon and Jimmy Kennedy)

Getting Oriented: "If you knew Susie like I know Suzie" (*If You Knew Susie* by Joseph Meyer and B.G. De Sylva) "They call me the great pretender" (*Great Pretender* by Buck Ram), "My funny valentine" (*My Funny Valentine,* from the musical *Babes in Arms* by Richard Rodgers and Lorenz Hart)

A Mine is a Terrible Thing: "Gonna take a sentimental journey. Gonna set my mind at ease" (*Sentimental Journey* by Les Brown and Ben Homer)

A Sonnet: "The song is ended, but the melody lingers on" *(The Song Is Ended* by Irving Berlin)

The Frown Princess: "Mighty like a rose" (*Mighty like a Rose* by Ethelbert Nevin and Frank L. Stanton)

Blimey! Slimy!: "A foggy day in London town" (*A Foggy Day in London Town* by George and Ira Gershwin)

Bag Lady: "Be it ever so humble, there's no place like home" (*Home Sweet Home* by Sir Henry Bishop)

San Simian: "Let a smile be your umbrella on a rainy, rainy day. If your sweetie cries, just tell her that a smile will always pay" (*Let a Smile Be Your Umbrella* by Sammy Fain, Irving Kahal, and Francis Wheeler)

Run of the Mill: "Down by the old mill stream" (*Down by the Old Mill Stream* by Tell Taylor)

Chapter 4

No Tunes Like Show Tunes

A Gem of a Romance

Once upon a slime, a girl ghoul fell in love with a mummy. Alas, the girl ghoul did not know much about the proper care of mummies, and in a couple of weeks the mummy began to unravel and disintegrated. Which just goes to prove that a ghoul and her mummy are soon parted.

Then the ghoul fell in love with a little devil, who turned out to be a loving and generous sweetheart. The little devil showered the girl ghoul with bright flowers, high-fashion clothes, and expensive jewelry. Which just goes to prove that *demons are a ghoul's best fiend.*

Get a Long, Little Stogie

Said Fidel to some girls in bandanas:
"I smoke, so I won't go bananas.
   Now my craving's acute,
   May I light this cheroot?"
Said the girls, *"Yes, we ban no Havanas."*

A Fairy Funny Story

The mayor of a small town favored a certain soft drink and drank it to the exclusion of all else, to the extent that he eventually acquired a nickname after this beverage.

That wasn't his most unusual quirk, though. Although the official was in many ways a dull fellow — slow and methodical — he had one other quirk besides his beverage preference that marked him as newsworthy, though at first it was a secret.

You see, many people in government keep pets — Socks, Buddy, or Checkers for example — but this mayor didn't keep an ordinary pet around his residence. Instead, he had a sprite whom he kept around for company. This magical being, who was blotchily multicolored, was kept hidden away from the public till, one day, a snooping reporter, prowling around the politician's residence, came upon the sprite. He asked, "Who are you?"

The creature replied, *"I am the fairy, mottled, of a ploddin' Mayor Gingerale."*

Art Attack

There is art on the wall (for a start);
Art archaic, like "Thou art so smart."
   Art is skill at a game,
   And there's Art, Carney's name;
So let's hit it!: *"You gotta have art!"*

Halitosis Diagnosis

Dr. Victor Frankenstein created creatures other than human monsters. He also specialized in creating large animals for meat production. His death occurred during the development of a hog weighing over two tons. The madman used almost 80 trained gorilla clones and one grizzly bear to carry out the mundane daily tasks of caring for this brute, who looked remarkably like Jabba the Hut.

One of the complicating factors in caring for this beast was his terrible bad breath. After feeding, it was necessary for several of the apes to force over a hundred Chlorets down his throat before anyone could go into the lab.

On the day of Dr. Frankenstein's death, one of the gorillas spilled the breath freshener tablets onto the floor. The mad scientist became enraged and began beating the poor ape. The ape's brothers went ape, and pandemonium ensued. It was four days before the police could enter the area. Portions of Dr. Frankenstein's remains were DNA-fingerprinted from wall and ceiling residue.

The police report summarizing the event concluded, *"Seventy-six strong clones fed the pig's bear aide, with a hundred and ten Clorets close at hand."*

Custard's Last Fling

It was an important day for my family. My aunt was getting married. I was six and was the ring bearer, and my eight-year-old sister was the flower girl. I was dressed in a tuxedo with bow tie and fancy shirt, and my sister was in a bridesmaid's gown. At the reception dinner, my sister would not stop teasing me, calling me Little Lord Fauntleroy and saying I looked like a sissy.

By the time dessert was served, I couldn't take it any longer. I picked up the dish and threw it at her, covering her with gooey sweets. To this day my sister reminds me that in front of all the guests *I'd thrown a custard in her face.*

Maintaining Their Equine-imity

At the 1992 Olympics in Barcelona, some of the locals were entered in equestrian events. Other contestants were surprised to note that the Spanish riders guided their horses with so much slack in the reins that they actually hung down across the horses' necks.

When asked why they preferred such a relaxed stance, the locals proudly explained, "*The reins in Spain fall plainly on the mane.*"

A Milestone, Not a Millstone

History was made in 2004, when the University of Connecticut's women's basketball squad defeated Tennessee in the national championship game, just a day after the men's team beat Georgia Tech in their final. It was the first time in NCAA history that men's and women's teams from the same school won the national championship in the same season. In commemoration of this feat, the school's music department wrote a variation on a classic song: *"Anything I can do, UConn do better."*

Annie Get Your Pun

The casting for *Annie* was done —
Not Orphan, but Oakley with gun.
   The actress, good looking,
   Enjoyed gourmet cooking
She could get a pan with a pun.

Director, a lecher named Mike,
Asked Annie out for a short hike,
   But he got no kissin' as
   He's now out of business.
A no-show's what her biz is like.

The Razors' Edge

As stories of outrageous graft grow more prevalent, more and more politicians in high station are getting dragged before judges and committees to defend themselves. Senator Bullwar Bilgebottom was accused of accepting thousands of dollars in illegal campaign contributions. His accusers claimed that the senator deviously accepted electric shavers in place of money and that those shavers were quickly sold for cash that found its way back to the senator's personal bank accounts. Senator Bilgebottom roundly protested, *"I get no Schicks from campaigns!"*

There's the Rub

Living in the modern world has resulted in stress and strain unknown to our ancestors. By the end of the day, accumulated tensions result in headaches, backaches, and other distressing symptoms. Many have found relief only from frequent treatments from masseurs and masseuses, practitioners who rub us the right way. They are *people who knead people*.

One masseuse fell in love with and started dating one of her male clients. As the relationship deepened, she constantly talked about "my boyfriend's trigger points," "my boyfriend's cervical spine," and "*my boyfriend's back*."

Light House Keeping

Some advice I got as a young 'un:
Not to stare at a lighthouse that's gleamin'
   'Cause a high power light
   Can damage your sight
When you peek in the beacon.

A Loony Idea

These days, commercial space tours have become a reality. If you can afford the tab and pass the physical, you can travel with NASA on a space flight around the earth.

The German government wants to take this development a step further and has funded the Omar Corporation to do the necessary research to build a domed vacation resort on the moon.

Venture capital has been solicited throughout the world to fund the construction of the resort to be ready for its grand opening by 2010.

The resort will cater to honeymoon couples and will have extensive sports and entertainment facilities, as well as Las Vegas-style casinos. It will be built on the near side of the moon so that guests will always have a view of the earth. The cost for a one week vacation is not known, but will certainly be expensive.

The Omar Corporation has already developed its

advertising campaign to promote the trips. The slogan will be *"A trip to the moon on Das Omar's wings — Must fun on those flings."*

Hair's a Pun for You

A traveler in the Himalayas came upon a great gathering of holy men, philosophers, and aspiring Buddhas. They represented all aspects of belief and seeking, including one aged guru who was reputed to have achieved nirvana by subsisting entirely on a diet of asparagus. Our traveler was astonished when, in a sudden mountain shower, all of the participants in this conclave were drenched, except the asparagus-eater. The rain simply avoided falling on him, as if he were roofed.

"That's incredible," said the traveler.

"Not at all," said his native guide. *"Bliss is the awning of the Sage of Asparagus."*

Surreality Show

It is a little known fact that a pharmacist was responsible for saving the career of the creator of surrealist paintings, Salvador Dali. It seems the artist accidentally poured boiling water on his drawing hand and immediately sought help at the local pharmacy. "What is the name of that medicinal plant that is good to treat burns?" Our hero replied, *"Aloe, Dali."*

Jest for the Health of It

Cartoon mom Marge Simpson and singing sensation Tina Turner opened up a health food restaurant together. Their menu selections were exceedingly tasty, even though the items were never cooked in a pan or breaded. Thus, it was never necessary for their customers to shout to the two owners, *"Don't fry for me, Marge and Tina!"*

Nobody Doesn't Like Our Show

Two major food companies were collaborating to sponsor and produce a TV special to advertise their new cooperative product — a cake-like treat made with the very best chocolate. The show was to feature good clean family entertainment, and the chosen M.C. was one of the most admired personalities in the business.

Unfortunately, as time for the live show grew near, the host's reputation began to tarnish in association with a growing scandal. The sponsors announced that they knew nobody who did not like the host and issued a strong denial: *"It taints Nestlé/Sara Lee Show. It taints Nestlé/Sara Lee Show. The things that you're liable to read, they are libel. It taints Nestlé/Sara Lee Show."*

A Song by George

It's fascinating to study how songwriters get their ideas for songs. This is the story about the origin of one of George Gershwin's biggest hits.

Dietary habits vary tremendously among cultures and can change drastically in any given group in a short period of time. We can see the velocity of such change from the recent rapid switch from low protein, high carbohydrate diets to control cholesterol to the high meat, low-carb Atkins and South Park diets to control obesity. Today, you will find meat at virtually every dinner, but it wasn't always this way.

Back in the early thirties, during the worst years of

the Great Depression (which really wasn't so great), meat was considered a sign of affluence, and no respectable dinner party would be without a proper serving of meat.

It so happened that the Gershwin family had invited a group of potential angels to a diner party at their home, when the chef notified Mrs. Gershwin that all their meat had spoiled because the ice man had failed to show up that day. Mrs. Gershwin panicked and sent George to the neighborhood butcher to obtain suitable meat to serve that evening.

When George arrived at the butcher shop, he found that they had not had a delivery of meat in several days and were completely out of most cuts. In fact, the butcher was getting ready to close his shop because he had so little to sell.

"You don't have any beef?" George asked.

"No, and we're completely out of pork, poultry, and even fish," he explained.

"Well, what do you have?" asked George.

And the butcher answered, *"I've got plenty of mutton."*

The Son Also Rises

Rachel came downstairs one morning in the little house in Anatevka. Jacob was sitting in a chair in the kitchen warming his toes by the fire. "Shall I make breakfast for you, my dearest Jacob?" asked Rachel.

"But of course," replied Jacob.

"And what of Mikhail and Aaron?" asked Rachel.

"They've already had their breakfast."

"So soon? But the sun isn't yet over the barn."

Answered Jacob, *"Sun rise, sons et."*

A Cereal Thriller

I knew I loved Teresa the moment I met her. She was intelligent, sweet, and witty — everything I had always desired. She was an executive with a major ad agency and had just sold Quaker Oats a new campaign for their healthy dry cereal. But we were separated in the crowd and I spent hours searching for her. Finally, I spotted her and loudly sang out: *"Ahh, sweet Miss Terry of LIFE, at last I've found you!"*

An Icicle Built for You

A grand state dinner was to take place in a South American country to honor the visiting prime minister of Israel, a former war hero. A noted sculptor was contracted to carve a frozen likeness of the Israeli dignitary surrounded by colorful birds that were native to the host country.

As the hour of the banquet drew near, the sculptor, having completed his frozen artwork, was relaxing in the walk-in freezer awaiting the moment when it would be practical to assemble his finished sculptures in the banquet hall.

To kill time, he began playing poker with some of the idle waiters and cooks. Just as a fresh round of cards had been dealt, the sculptor received a message on his pager. He suddenly rose up from the table, offered his cards to a nearby kitchen worker, and exclaimed, *"Take my hand. I must arrange Sharon parrot ice."*

Over a Carol

Three young men, filled with Christmas cheer, decided to serenade a number of their female acquaintances with songs of the season.

At Betty's house they sang the mistress's anthem, "God Rest Ye Married, Gentlemen," and Betty welcomed the gesture warmly with a round of eggnog.

Encouraged, the trio moved on to Alice's house, where they crooned the lament of the cherubs under stress, "Hark, The Harried Angels Sing!" Alice rewarded the singers with glasses of steaming punch.

Buoyed by the spirit of the moment, the troubadours stopped next at Ina's house. Unfortunately, no one was home. Keen to have her hear them, yet feeling somewhat fatigued by their musical efforts, the leader suggested that they return the next day. "After all," he observed. "We can always *carol Ina in the morning.*"

The Answers, My Friends

A Gem of a Romance: "Diamonds are a girl's best friend" (*Diamonds are a Girl's Best Friend,* from *Gentlemen Prefer Blondes* by Jule Styne and Leo Robin)

Get a Long, Little Stogie: "Yes, we have no bananas" (*Yes! We Have No Bananas,* from *Make It Snappy* by Frank Silver and Irving Cohn)

A Fairy Funny Story: "I am the very model of a modern major-general," (*I am the Modern of a Modern Major-General,* from *The Pirates of Penzance* by Arthur S. Sullivan and W.S. Gilbert)

Art Attack: "You gotta have heart" (*You Gotta Have Heart,* from *Damn Yankees* by Richard Adler and Jerry Ross)

Halitosis Diagnosis: "Seventy-six trombones led the big parade. With a hundred and ten cornets close at hand" (*Seventy-Six Trombones,* from *The Music Man by* Meredith Wilson)

Custard's Last Fling: "I've grown accustomed to her face" (*I've Grown Accustomed to Her Face,* from *My Fair Lady* by Frederick Loewe and Alan Jay Lerner)

Maintaining Their Equine-imity: "The rain in Spain falls mainly on the plain" (*The Rain in Spain,* from *My Fair Lady)*

A Milestone, Not a Millstone: "Anything you can do I can do better" (*Anything You Can Do,* from *Annie Get Your Gun* by Irving Berlin)

Annie Get Your Pun: "You can't get a man with a gun" *(You Can't Get a Man with a Gun)* and "There's no business like show business" *(There's No Business like Show Business,* from *Annie Get Your Gun)*

The Razors' Edge: "I get no kicks from champagne" (*I Get a Kick out of You,* from *Anything Goes* by Cole Porter)

There's the Rub: "People who need people" (*People,* from *Funny Girl,* by Bob Merrill and Jule Styne) and "My boyfriend's back" (*My Boyfriend's Back* by Robert Feldman, Gerald Goldstein, and Richard Gottehre)

Light House Keeping: "When we begin the beguine" (*Begin the Beguine,* from *Jubilee* by Cole Porter)

A Loony Idea: "A trip to the moon on gossamer wings – Just one of those things" (*Just One of Those Things,* from *Jubilee)*

Hair's a Pun for You: "This is the dawning of the age of Aquarius" (*This is the Dawning of the Age of Aquarius,* from *Hair* by Galt McDermot, James Rado, and Gerome Ragni)

Surreality Show: "Hello, Dolly" (*Hello Dolly,* from *Hello, Dolly* by Jerry Herman)

Jest for the Health of It: "Don't cry for me, Argentina" (*Don't Cry for Me, Argentina,* from *Evita* by Andrew Lloyd Webber and Tim Rice*)*

Nobody Doesn't Like Our Show: "It ain't necessarily so. It ain't necessarily so. The things that you're liable to read in the Bible, they ain't necessarily so" (*It Ain't Necessarily So,* from *Porgy and Bess* by George Gershwin, DuBose Heyward, and Ira Gershwin)

A Song by George: "I got plenty of nothin'" (*I Got Plenty o' Nothin',* from *Porgy and Bess*)

The Son Also Rises: "Sunrise, sunset" (*Sunrise, Sunset,* from *Fiddler on the Roof* by Sheldon Harnick and Jerry Bock)

Cereal Thriller: "Ah, sweet mystery of life, at last I've found you" (*Ah! Sweet Mystery of Life,* from *Naughty Marietta* by Victor Herbert and Rida Johnson Young)

An Icicle Built for You: "Take my hand. I'm a stranger in paradise" (*Stranger in Paradise,* from *Kismet,* by Robert Wright and George Forrest, based on music by Alexander Borodin)

*Over a Carol: "*Carolina in the Morning" (*Carolina in the Morning*, from *The Passing Show of 1922* by Walter Donaldson and Gus Kahn)

Chapter 5

No Tunes Like Show Tunes 2
Rodgers and Hammerstein Revue

Bring on the Clones

In this modern era, where cloning and genetic engineering have become household words, few of us remember the true pioneer of genetic experimentation — Dr. Moreau. Not the Dr. Moreau immortalized by H. G. Wells in his famous novel, but the real Pierre Moreau, who actually attempted to form new species from unrelated animals. Most of his experiments failed. Most of the documents that survived deal with his attempts to cross an owl and a goat to create a hootenanny, but none lived more than a few hours after birth. His studies were ridiculed by the French Academy of Science, and he died in disgrace, not realizing he was a hundred years ahead of his time.

He had only a single real success, which occurred when he crossed the chromosomes of the black rhinoceros with the giant panda of China. Only one of this new species, which he called a pandaceros, but playfully called a furry, survived beyond infancy, but with diligence and care, it did grow to full maturity.

This magnificent animal was over five feet tall and weighed 500 pounds. The creature sported a long black and white fur coat and an 18-inch hollow cylindrical horn on its forehead. The horn communicated through a canal with the posterior pharynx, which, unlike the elephant, which uses its trunk to breathe, was primary used for feeding.

The furry's daily supply of bamboo shoots and berries was placed in the horn, and with the use of a plunger-like devise invented by Dr. Moreau, the beast could get its frequent feedings as it desired. It was a loving animal, ideal for a pet, and loved to play with children. Unfortunately, like most hybrids, it was sterile. This made commercial production of pandaceri uneconomical, and the process was never repeated by Dr. Moreau or his disciples.

In 1895, faced with forced closure of his island laboratories, Dr. Moreau sold his only successful hybrid to the Circus de Royal, where it was the premier attraction for two years before its untimely death from pneumonia. Visitors from throughout the world traveled to pet this wonderful beast and place food on its horn, which the hybrid would joyfully – but often unhealthily suck down. For a few years, the Circus de Royal was the most talked about and visited entertainment center in all of Europe.

Now, more than a hundred years after the untimely death of the world's only pandaceros, no one remains alive who can remember trips to the circus and the excitement of seeing and petting the magnificent *furry with the syringe on top.*

The Windy City

A handsome young man was walking down a road in Yokohama, Japan. Suddenly a powerful wind came up and swirled around the fellow. Eddies of wind seemed to jump into his clothing, puffing out this garments. He was not at all surprised because he knew about *Yokohama, where the wind comes leaping down the swain.*

A Grave Situation

Though the young fellow's mom had just died, he couldn't afford to miss a day at work. The restaurant manager insisted he show up or be fired. So he did the best he could, deciding to honor his late parent with a black armband over his uniform. And not just any black armband. This one was elegant silk, with ornate decorations on it.

It caught the attention of the customers at one of his tables, who commented, *"Oh, waiter, beautiful mourning."*

A Garden-Variety Disease

In the wealthy suburbs of Palm Springs, a strange malady was striking the gardeners on the large estates. They were becoming morose and depressed, and had to be hospitalized. The first signs of the disease were when they started complaining that the lawns were in terrible shape.

A psychiatrist brought in to find out what was happening noticed that there were some gardeners who still remained cheerful and never developed the lawn-hating symptoms. The psychiatrist went over and over this group, trying to find out why they were immune and what they were doing differently.

Finally, he noticed that the healthy gardeners always had garden twine in the wheelbarrow, whereas the sick gardeners carried the roll in their pockets. So then the cure was obvious: *"Walk on, walk on, with rope in your cart, and you'll never knock a lawn."*

Put Through the Mill

Lowell, Massachusetts, is an old New England mill town. Many of the mills have been declared national historical sites and are included in a federal park. The problem was what to do with the other mills, and how to attract more tourists to the area.

One bright young marketer pointed out that Germans like to travel with their dogs, and this was difficult in the United States. "Why not make the mills into canine hotels?" he suggested. The plan was adopted on a trial basis, but not without some skepticism.

Several months later, the skeptics approached the young man to ask how the experiment was going.

"Just listen!" he said, *"The mills are alive with the hounds of Munich!"*

Picking up Ascent

A climbing team set out to reach the top of a treacherous mountain, which had never been successfully scaled. As they neared the summit, they were surprised to encounter a bunch of clowns who lived together in a village.

On the outskirts of the clown village, high in the clouds, they came to a fork in the trail, the two paths quickly disappearing in the thick clouds. One trail led to the summit, but the other led right off the edge of a 500-foot cliff. The team leader asked the clowns which path in the fork the climbers should take. The clowns all pointed to the one on the right. The leader figured that a bunch of clown villagers were just clowning around, so he turned to his team and promptly led them down the other trail. Unfortunately, in the thick clouds they never saw the edge of the cliff until they had already fallen off it.

As the echoes of their screams slowly faded away, the clowns sadly shook their funny heads and sighed, "After all these years, you'd think they would have learned by now to *mind every clown town.*"

The Party Invitation

Daisy was recently divorced by her husband of twenty years. He had been having an affair with his secretary, she had become pregnant, and he wanted to marry her.

The newly single Daisy decided that the next man she would marry would have to be one who worked in parks and watched out for fires.

One day Daisy received a formal engraved invitation from Janet and Samuel Rosen to attend their gala fifteenth wedding anniversary party. She didn't know the Rosens very well, but she decided that she would attend when a friend told her that "at a *Sam and Janet evening, you will see a ranger.*"

A Punny Bunny Story

When I was six, Mommy gave me an Easter bunny, and it was my responsibility to take care of him. I called him Fluffy because he had long hair and was fluffy just like my favorite stuffed animals. The only problem was his fluffy fur caught everything it came into contact with — leaves, feathers, food, you name it. If he rubbed against it, it stuck to him. So I spent most of the day combing all the foreign bodies out of his fur. It seemed I had to comb him twenty to thirty times a day.

One morning when my mother was making pancakes, my four-year-old sister, Jill, asked Mommy about the oil she poured into the skillet before putting the batter on. Mommy told her it was to prevent the food from sticking to the pan,

Well, Jill had a great idea. She would spread the magic liquid all over Fluffy's fur so the food and other substances wouldn't stick to him.

When I went to Fluffy's cage, I found he was no longer Fluffy. He looked emaciated with his fur plastered against his skin. I rushed into Mommy's room and asked her what to do. She came up with a simple solution.

As I was carrying Fluffy into the bathroom, Jill in tears came up to me and asked me what I was going to do. I told her, *"I'm gonna wash that PAM right out of my hare!"*

SWAT's it All About?

Amidst a dramatic hostage situation unfolding in a bank in downtown Boston, the Commissioner summoned the head of the Police Department SWAT team. "Analysis has shown that the guy is generally visible from the window of an office on the thirty-second floor of the building diagonally across the street. Do you have someone available who can place a shot from there?"

"Well," replied Captain O'Reilly, "We have Crazy Louie in the precinct today. Probably the best on our team. I'll call him in."

While Maintenance cut a section of glass from the window, Louie lay out on a table, on his back, head toward the window. Holding his rifle in the air, pointing downward over his shoulder and out the window, he sighted into a mirror on the stock, ever so gently squeezed the trigger, and on a single shot brought down the culprit.

Details of the incident quickly leaked to the press. "How could you possibly make a shot like that? Isn't this somewhat unconventional?"

"Aw, shucks," replied Louie. *"There is nothing you can name that is anything like odd aim."*

The Answers, My Friends

Bring on the Clones: "The surrey with the fringe on top" (*The Surrey with the Fringe on Top,* from *Oklahoma!*)

The Windy City: "Oklahoma, where the wind goes sweeping down the lane" (*Oklahoma!,* from *Oklahoma!*)

A Grave Situation: "Oh, what a beautiful morning" (*Oh, What a Beautiful Morning,* from *Oklahoma!*)

A Garden-Variety Disease: "Walk on, walk on with hope in your heart, and you'll never walk alone" (*You'll Never Walk Alone,* from *Carousel*)

Put Through the Mill: "The hills are alive with the sound of music" (*The Sound of Music,* from *The Sound of Music*)

Picking up Ascent: "Climb every mountain" (*Climb Ev'ry Mountain,* from *The Sound of Music*)

The Party Invitation "Some enchanted evening, you may see a stranger" (*Some Enchanted Evening,* from *South Pacific*)

A Punny Bunny Story: "I'm gonna wash that man right outa my hair" (*I'm Gonna Wash That Man Right outa My Hair,* from *South Pacific*)

SWAT's It All About?: "There is nothing you can name that is anything like a dame" (*Nothing like a Dame,* from *South Pacific*)

Chapter 6

Movie Tune News

A Frog in Your Throat

In the wonderful Land of Oz, Dorothy, the Scarecrow, the Tin Man, and the Cowardly Lion made their way from one exhilarating and exhausting adventure to another. Seeking a break from their intense lives, they took up the pastime of toad licking. They found that licking the toads native to the Emerald City made them feel happy and self-confident, and especially relaxed.

After running their tongues over the skin of one particular amphibian, Dorothy and her friends experienced an incredibly peaceful state of well being. So for the rest of their stay in Oz, the girl, the scarecrow, the heavy metal fellow, and the lion would *follow the mellow licked toad.*

A New-Fashioned Girl

A popular talk show hostess introduced a line of women's clothing. It was a very complete line from casual to formal and featured a wide variety of fabrics and colors. As she watched the new spring line being modeled for her and her staff, she turned to one of her staff and asked which one she had liked the best. They replied, *"Sun wear, Oprah, the rayon blue."*

The Drunk Backs of Notre Dame

The Notre Dame football coach was having a problem with some of his players. Most adhered strictly to training rules, but a few would take advantage of the welcoming taverns in the town and occasionally sneak some drinks.

One night, the coach, anxious because some of his players were missing during bed check, made the rounds of the local pubs to search for them. Just as he entered one bar, two of his star players, the quarterback and fullback, spotted him and tried to sneak off into the lavatory.

What'll it be?" bartender asked the coach.

"Just a Coke for me," replied the coach, " but *see what the backs in the boys room will have."*

Quit While You're a Head

There once was a medieval village that was being terrorized by a vile monster. The creature was called the Head of Sin because its awful head looked like a devil's face. Each night, the Head of Sin would slither down from the hills and devour one of the villagers. The terrified citizenry called a meeting, and decided to pool their money to hire the great hero Erik.

Erik came and listened to the complaints of the villagers. He consulted his *Great Hero's Book of Vile Monsters* and learned that the Head of Sin loved to eat loons. So Erik captured a loon, tied it up, and brought it back to the village. He then had the villagers dig a deep pit. Erik threw the loon into the pit, hoping to capture the monster and slay it.

That night, the Head of Sin crawled to the edge of the pit. It smelled the loon, but the creature also smelled danger, and it ran off, devouring one of the villagers on the way out.

After calming the villagers the next day, Erik again consulted his *Great Hero's Book of Vile Monsters* and learned that the Head of Sin also loved sugar. So Erik gathered up all of the sugar in the village and threw it into the pit. The loon, not having eaten in days, devoured all of the sugar in a single gulp. Erik was struck with panic and ran to and fro, trying to figure out what to do next. But night had fallen, and the Head of Sin would be there soon. Erik crossed his fingers and hoped for the best.

That night, the Head of Sin came. It smelled the loon. It smelled danger, but it also smelled the sugar. The Head of Sin quickly slithered down into the pit and devoured the loon. The villagers swarmed over the murderous Head and slew it. Which goes to show that *a loon full of sugar helps the Head of Sin go down*.

Egyptian Conniption

Long ago, the Egyptian queen Cleopatra made an asp of herself. To explain: Cleopatra decided to commit suicide by clasping a small cobra, called an asp, to her bosom. She selected an asp with especially long teeth because she wanted to die from the sharpest *fangs for the mammary.*

Making a Point

William B. was the founder of Alcoholics Anonymous. One day, he and his girlfriend Kay were exploring the wonders of the Louvre museum in Paris, when they came upon the museum's famous collection of French Impressionist art.

Suddenly William, unfamiliar as he was with the fine points of the period, came across a well-known painting that he mistakenly thought was an example of pointillism. He immediately called his wife over and naively exclaimed, *"Kay, Seurat! Seurat!"*

She took one bored look at the painting and replied, *"Whatever, Will B., Will B."*

Humor in a Jugular Vein

We all love to travel, and vampires, too, need their rest and relaxation. So Count Dracula went on a tour of Europe. Having not had a meal since he'd left the homeland of Transylvania, he was very glad when a town constable knocked on his hotel door and asked the count to show him his passport. It didn't take Dracula long to grab the policemen and suck every drop of blood out of him.

Now Dracula was faced with a problem. "How do I dispose of this body?" he wondered. The only solution he could come with was to throw the corpse out the window "I'm so high up, they'll never trace the body back to me. Ha ha," he cackled. So – whoosh – out the window went the corpse.

It just so happened that right below that window was the customary station of an itinerant street singer. Bang! The singer got hit right on his noggin by the falling body and was knocked unconscious.

Back in his hotel room Dracula was in the mood for "dessert," so he rang room service and asked the front desk to send up another town constable. Ten minutes later the policeman arrived and Dracula invited him in.

As soon as the door shut, Dracula pounced and devoured his fresh and steaming "dessert." Again the count wondered "How do I get rid of the body?" and then thought, "Well, it worked once. Why not again?" So out the window went his latest victim.

At that moment the street singer below had just regained consciousness and was wondering what the heck was going on. His consciousness didn't last long, however, as he was instantly knocked out cold by Count Dracula's second victim.

Some time later the singer woke up and saw that a small crowd had gathered around. As he regained his bearings, one of the onlookers asked, "What's happened here?"

"It's terrible," sang the street singer. *"Drained cops keep falling on my head!"*

Frankly Speaking

Many people are unaware that singer Frank Sinatra was also an ecologist. He found out that the herds of wildebeests in Africa were being forced off their native lands into game reserves where they were more apt to be eaten by their natural enemies due to the crowded conditions.

These animals would congregate around lakes and other bodies of water, but had nowhere to run if they were attacked by their foes. This resulted in abnormal losses in the herds.

Frank, upon finding out about this, donated a lot of money to find open land for the animals so they wouldn't be so crowded. Sinatra's idea was to go to the watering holes and load the wildebeests onto large barges and take them to the other lands and set them free.

In order to accomplish this, he had to finance his work through a best-selling song about it. We've all heard the song before. It begins *"Start spreading the gnus."* The title of the song is, of course, *"New Ark, New Ark."*

Aardvark and No Play

Knock, knock.
Who's there?
Aardvark.
Aardvark who?
Aardvark a million miles for one of your smiles.

Once Pawn a Time

England's King Edward VII was alarmed when his admirals informed him that Kaiser Wilhelm was embarking on a crash building course to greatly increase the Imperial German Fleet. When he asked how much money would be required to build a dreadnought that would defeat the German Navy, the admiralty informed him, "100 million pounds sterling, your majesty."

"Oh dear me, I'll have to pawn the Star of India, the largest diamond in the world, the front piece on the Crown Royal to pay for this!"

"Dedication, your majesty" was all they could reply.

So the King sent for the Crown Royal and person-ally dug out the Star of India and took it in the state carriage to a pawnbroker in the East End, where he'd seen such establishments.

"How much will you give me for the Star of India, my good man?"

"Ow, Guv'nuh, Oi t'ink all I kin lend ye would be 100 pounds."

"What? A mere 100 pounds sterling! This is the Star of India, worth 10,000 times that. Do you know who I am?"

The pawnbroker replied, *"When you wish to pawn a star, makes no difference who you are."*

On a Roll

Have you ever wondered what happened to Snow White and the seven vertically challenged people she lived with? Well, eventually the diamond mine stopped producing gems and their revenue stream started drying up.

One evening at dinner, Snow White and her seven buddies were talking about how they could earn some money. Lots of different ideas were proposed for a new venture, but nothing clicked.

"Here's a suggestion," offered Doc, the wisest of the group. "Let's open up a 1-hour photo service. I've seen them in a lot of drugstores and they seem to be doing a great business."

Doc and Happy (he's the one who is technically astute) did some research and ordered the latest in fast photo developing equipment. They rented a store in the local town, had the equipment sent there, set it up and opened the door for business. To capitalize on her fame, they called the business

Snow White's 1-Hour Photo Service. People flocked to the store.

The only problem was that business was too good and they couldn't fulfill the promise of one-hour service. As a matter of fact, they were getting so far behind in their work that it took almost a week for them to fulfill a film order.

The lack of timeliness was noted and one of their customers suggested a logo for the business: *"Some day my prints will come."*

On a Role

Actor Richard Crenna has starred in many TV series, including "The Real McCoys" and "Our Miss Brooks," as well as appearing in many motion pictures. However, he would be the first to tell you that he is best remembered for his part in an adventure trilogy. In fact, if you asked him which role was most instrumental in his career, he would burst into song: *"I'm Always Chasing Rambos."*

This Little Piggy

Medically these days, we have to worry not only about human diseases, but diseases of our companion and service animals, such as bird flu. The possibility of the prions responsible for mad cow disease being transmitted to humans is of considerable recent notoriety in the media. Iowa pig farmers have an additional worry — that the mad cow disease may be transmitted to pigs resulting in mad pig disease. In other words, they are worried about *the daze of swine neurosis.*

The Human Stain

Fred Astaire and Ginger Rogers were having dinner at an expensive New York restaurant. It was the place to be seen and both had dressed for the occasion. Ginger was resplendent in a ball gown and diamond tiara while Fred wore his smartest morning suit. But the evening was marred when the waiter bringing their desserts tripped and covered Fred from head to toe in treacle sponge.

"I'm terribly sorry," said the red-faced waiter.

"You should be," grumped Fred. "Thanks to you *I've pudding on my top hat, pudding on my white tie, pudding on my tails!"*

A Brand New Name

Major advertising agencies usually have a special department whose only task is to find the best name for a new product, one that will catch the public eye.

One such band of professional brand namers was sitting around a table working on a big commission. A major chemical company was paying them big bucks to come up with a moniker for its new insecticide.

"Let's call it Bug Beheader," suggested one member of the brain-storming team.

"No, let's call it Bugs Begone," rejoined a second member.

But the third of the group won the day with *"Let's call the whole thing OFF!"*

Making an Impression

A wealthy art critic so hated the works of a particular French impressionist that he made it his mission in life to buy up all his paintings and smash them into to pieces on top of a pile of hard volcanic rock. So passionately obsessed was he by this quest that his motto became, *"Lava's a Manet splintered thing."*

Tank You

Henri LeCoq, Ph.D., was a staff scientist at the National Fish Hatchery and Research Institute. He had spent a long career studying the physiology of fish and was recognized as *the* international expert in the oxygen transfer process through the gills. Much of his research was carried out by a flock of assistants, graduate students, and technicians. An entire section of his laboratory was supported and staffed by private industry, which used his research results in the development of commercial films for osmosis and transpiration. The research areas included not only the biological and physical mechanisms of breathing, but also the genetics of the organs.

Which brings us to the "sorting room," wherein the fish (guppies, in this case, due to a quick life cycle) were being categorized by gill size. An assistant was removing a couple of guppies from each tank, taking a few critical measurements and returning the fish to the tank. She quickly noted that some of the small-gilled fish were in the wrong tank. A quick look at the records indicated that Ralph was doing the sorting that week — and it was not the first time he had erred.

At this moment Dr. LeCoq happened by and inquired as to the problem. When told what had transpired, he slapped his forehead. "Mon Dieu," he exclaimed. "That boy can't follow directions!" They summoned Ralph to the lab, and all LeCoq could say to him was, *"Tank Seven for little gills!"*

The Answers, My Friends

A Frog in Your Throat: "Follow the yellow-brick road" (*We're Off To See The Wizard* by Harold Arlen and E.Y. Harburg, from *The Wizard of Oz)*

A New-Fashioned Girl: "Somewhere over the rainbow" (*Over the Rainbow,* from *The Wizard of Oz)*

Quit While You're a Head: "Just a spoonful of sugar makes the medicine go down" (*A Spoonful of Sugar* by Richard M. Sherman and Robert B. Sherman, from *Mary Poppins)*

The Drunk Backs of Notre Dame: "See what the boys in the back room will have" ("Boys in The Backroom" by Frank Loesser, from *The Moon of Manakonna)*

Egyptian Conniption: "Thanks for the memory" (*Thanks for the Memory* by Ralph Rainger and Leo Robin, from *The Big Broadcast of 1938)*

Making a Point: "Que sera, sera. Whatever will be will be" (*Que Sera, Sera* by Jay Livingston and Ray Evans, from *The Man Who Knew Too Much)*

Humor in a Jugular Vein: "Raindrops keep falling on my head" (*Raindrops Keep Falling on My Head* by Burt Bacharach and Hal David, from *Butch Cassidy and the Sundance Kid)*

Frankly Speaking: "Start spreading the news," "New York, New York" (*New York, New York* by Leonard Bernstein and Adolph Green and Betty Green, from *On the Town)*

Aardvark and No Play: "I'd walk a million miles for one of your smiles" (*My Mammy* by Walter Donaldson, Sam M. Lewis, and Joe Young, from *The Jazz Singer)*

Once Pawn a Time: "When you wish upon a star, makes no difference who you are" (*When You Wish upon a Star* by Leigh Harline and Ned Washington, from *Snow White and the Seven Dwarfs*)

On a Roll: "Some day my prince will come" (*Someday My Prince will Come* by Frank Churchill and Larry Morey, from *Snow White and the Seven Dwarfs*);

On a Role: "I'm always chasing rainbows" (*I'm Always Chasing Rainbows,* by Henry Carroll and Joseph McCarthy, from *The Dolly Sisters*)

This Little Piggy: "The days of wine and roses" (*The Days of Wine and Roses* by Henry Mancini and Johnny Mercer, from *Days of Wine and Roses*)

The Human Stain: "I'm putting on my top hat, tying on my white tie, brushing off my tails" (*My Top Hat* by Irving Berlin, from *Top Hat*)

A Brand New Name: "Let's call the whole thing off" (*Let's Call The Whole Thing Off* by George and Ira Gershwin, from *Shall We Dance?*)

Making an Impression: "Love is a many-splendored thing" (*Love Is a Many-Splendored Thing* by Sammy Fain and Paul Frances Webster, from *Love Is a Many-Splendored Thing*)

Tank You: "Thank heaven for little girls" (*Thank Heaven for Little Girls* by Frederick Loewe and Alan Jay Lerner, from *Gigi*)

Chapter 7

Child's Play

An Age-Old Story

Millions of people around the world have sat transfixed for hours in theaters and enjoyed that peculiar conspiracy of light and darkness and sound we call the movies. Many an actor and actress has captured our hearts and then grown old and disappeared from our sight and hearts. Hollywood producers are cruel and do not suffer gladly the passage of time that writes itself on the faces of matinee idols. These once gorgeous men and women brighten the screen and our lives and then flame out like meteors.

Sometimes a movie fan will wonder, *"Wrinkle, wrinkle, brittle star. Now I wonder where you are."*

Cheese It

The astronauts in the Sea of Tranquility were amazed to discover that the moon actually did contain large underground deposits of cheese. Once outside the landing module, they climbed into the rover and drove across the lunar surface to obtain samples.

In one location they discovered a large deposit of brie and collected twenty-five pounds to bring back to earth. They drove to a second location and collected fifty pounds of camembert. In a third location they hit a vein of cheddar and collected another fifty pounds of samples.

Mission Control crackled through their headsets that it would not be satisfied unless they brought back at least another twenty-five pounds of brie. The astronauts turned their rover around and proceeded to the first location, where they collected another twenty-five pounds of the cheese.

The astronauts were almost back to the landing module when Mission Control radioed that it wanted another twenty-five pounds of brie.

Disgruntled, one of the astronauts sarcastically snapped into his microphone, *"Have you ever seen such a site in all your life as brie mined thrice?"*

The Flea Circuit

Antiques enthusiast Mary spent all her free time haunting second-hand stores, flea markets, and other likely spots where she might encounter the odd find: a valuable antique of some sort, whose seller was unaware of its value and was offering it for a low price.

On most of her expeditions she came up empty, but she enjoyed the thrill of the hunt and felt amply rewarded when she did manage to purchase a valuable old something-or-other from its unwitting seller.

On one such expedition, buried in the back of a thrift shop, Mary encountered a small, old-fashioned kerosene lighting device. Her heart leapt at the sight of it; she was sure it was worth considerably more than the dollar on the price tag.

Unfortunately, though, her newest find was infested with small albino insects that had jumped from the store's feline. She bought it all the same, though.

Now *Mary had a little lamp. Its fleas were white as snow.*

Pulling Our Eyes over the Wool

A very fussy fellow with a maniacal attention to detail one day decided to host a costume party. Characteristically, he insisted that all costumes be correct in all technical aspects. The night of the party, he stationed himself by the door of his mansion along with his butler, a rather burly fellow who tonight was doubling as bouncer. Any guest whose costume was deemed to be inaccurate, incomplete, or otherwise unsatisfactory was denied admission.

Along came the host's friend Barbara, dressed in an old-fashioned little-girl's outfit. The host scowled. "Who are you supposed to be?" he demanded.

"Little Bo-Peep," she answered demurely.

The host looked behind her and all around, scowled even more deeply, and turned to the butler-cum-bouncer and imperiously ordered, *"Bar Barb — lacks sheep."*

True Blue

A little-known canine companion of Mister Rogers was his trusty coon dog, Blue. Whenever Mister Rogers came home, Blue would let out the most beautiful, mournful wail of greeting. Faithful Blue never missed a single day of his hound hellos. Sometimes visitors would ask Mister Rogers what he thought about Blue's gritty greeting. Mister Rogers would gaze at Blue, smile warmly, and quietly say, *"It's a dutiful bay in the neighborhood."*

Playing Keep-Frog

Christmas was coming, and the Smith children insisted that Santa leave a present for their puppy, Skippy. So the next morning Dad stopped at Joe Saunders' pet store to purchase a doggie toy.

Joe told Mr. Smith that he had just purchased the inventory of a shop across town that had gone out of business. He now had a barrel of stuffed animals in the back that he had not yet had time to price. Joe said that if Dad picked a toy from there, it would be a great bargain.

When Mr. Smith went to the back, an eight-inch green frog immediately caught his eye. The toy looked almost real, was cuddly soft, and, when squeezed, made a loud croaking sound that could be heard across the store.

Mr. Smith decided this toy would be perfect for the family puppy, so he asked the proprietor, *"How much for that froggy in the bin, Joe?"*

Playing to Beat the Band

An elementary school music teacher was trying to teach her students the various kinds of music, from classical to rock to opera to folk to the blues to gospel. The school administrators discouraged loud noise in the classrooms and had forbidden the music teacher to use the tambourines and triangles and bells she had formerly used in class. Nonetheless, she wanted the kids to have some kind of "instruments" with which they could express themselves and feel the rhythm.

Accordingly, she had devised a homemade bow made of a tree branch and a thick rubber band, which, when struck, produced only a soft sound, one she hoped would not bring the wrath of the school authorities on her.

At the beginning of the class, she passed out a bow to each kid. "Now, this beat is called a tango," she explained, playing a bit of tango music on the boom-box she had brought into the classroom. "Do you like the tango? Let your fingers dance on your desktops if you can imagine yourself dancing to this tune.

"This is a march," she continued, cueing up another song. "If you feel the beat, march in place to the music.

"And this," she said before the third selection, "is something I'm sure you're all familiar with — rap. *If you're rappy and you know it, snap your bands.*"

Egging Them On

For more than forty years, Captain Finn Sharkey combed the seas for the highest-quality fish eggs. His harvest usually ended up as gourmet caviar at select tables in five-star restaurants around the world. Nothing would stop him from his search, even the most dreadful weather conditions, conditions that would keep other fishing boats tied up on shore. Whenever his craft encountered such a storm, Finn would urge his crew to work hard and *"boat, boat, boat your roe!"*

Comb, Sweet Comb

Did you hear about the wedding of Yves Montand and Carmen Miranda? It was a wedding combining many of the traditions of both of their heritages. Carmen's hair was worn up and held in place by beautiful, ornamental combs. After the vows, Carmen pulled out the combs, let her hair down, and combed it out as an act of submission, thereby concluding the ceremony and becoming his wife. Or, as the related tradition says, *"She'll be Carmen Miranda Montand when she combs."*

He's Not a Loafer

The owner of a highly successful bakery decided that he wanted to automate his system. He went shopping for a machine that would slice the loaves. First he inspected a machine that would slice one loaf at a time. Then his eyes lit upon a multi-bladed machine that would slice two loaves at once. He was surprised to come upon an advanced version that would slice three loaves at once. Still not satisfied, he wired back to the home office, *"I'm looking over a four-loaf cleaver."*

Sea the World

On a recent trip to SeaWorld, we were particularly impressed by the "Penguin Encounter." We looked all over the enclosure to see all the little penguins and puffins. Down at the far end there was a little male puffin in a lady's dress, pulling rabbits out of a hat, and performing all sorts of other tricks. We called him *Drag, the Magic Puffin.*

Old Timers Disease

The small hamlet of Earl Grey in Wales has been manufacturing great tea for more than fifty years. The town has also been re-electing the same mayor for decades. Although the mayor is senile and in her dotage, she is beloved and continues to win.

Lately she has been falling asleep during town

meetings and committee meetings, and sometimes she even forgets where she is or who she is. She rambles on in her speeches, forgets what she is saying, and, in short, is a disgrace and embarrassment to her position. The residents all agree that as lovable as she is, *the Earl Grey mayor just ain't what she used to be.*

The Answers, My Friends

Cheese It: "Have you ever seen such a sight in your life as three blind mice?" (*Three Blind Mouse,* traditional)

The Flea Circuit: "Mary had a little lamb. Its fleece was white as snow" (*Mary Had a Little Lamb* by Sarah Josepha Hale)

Pulling Our Eyes over the Wool: "Baa, Baa, black sheep" (*Baa, Baa, Black Sheep,* traditional)

An Age-Old Story: "Twinkle, twinkle, little star. How I wonder what you are" (*The Star,* traditional; same tune as *Baa. Baa, Black Sheep*, as well as *The Alphabet Song*)

True Blue: "It's a beautiful day in the neighbor-hood" title (*Won't You Be My Neighbor?* by Fred McFeely Rogers)

Playing Keep-Frog: "How much is that doggy in the window?" (*How Much Is That Doggy in the Win-dow?* by Bob Merrill)

Playing to Beat the Band: "If you're happy and you know it, clap your hands" (*If You're Happy and You Know It,* traditional)

Comb, Sweet Comb: "She'll be coming around the mountain when she comes" (*Coming 'Round the Mountain,* traditional)

Egging Them On: "Row, row, row your boat," *Row, Row Row Your Boat,* traditional)

He's Not a Loafer: "I'm looking over a four-leaf clover" (*I'm Looking over a Four-Leaf Clover* by Harry Woods and Mort Dixon)

Sea the World: "Puff, the magic dragon" (*Puff [the Magic Dragon]* by Peter Yarnow and Leonard Lipton)

Old Timers Disease: "The old gray mare just ain't what she used to be" (*The Old Gray Mare,* tradi-tional)

Chapter 8

Sense and Nonsense

You Can Bank on It

This frog was really down on his luck. All he had left in the world was a little ceramic figurine his mother had willed him when she croaked. So he decided he'd go to the bank and get a loan so he could improve his lot in life. He wrapped up the figurine and hopped on down to the local bank.

When he got to the bank, the bank receptionist directed him to a loan officer by the name of Patricia Whack. Ms. Whack took one look at the frog, and knew her day was ruined. "Okay," she said, "what can I do for you?"

"Well, I'd like a small loan," the frog said, "So I can get back on my feet."

The loan officer found this a little odd, but got out

a form. "Okay, what's your name?"

The frog answered, "Kermit Jagger."

"Really? Any relation to Mick Jagger?"

"Yeah, he's my dad."

"We don't usually loan money to frogs," Patty said. "Do you have any collateral?"

The frog held up the figurine and said, "Well, I have this."

Patty rolled her eyes. "I'm going to have to ask my manager."

She went to find the manager, and told him, "You're not going to believe this. There's this frog out here who says he's Mick Jagger's son. He wants a loan, and his only collateral is this little figurine. Have you ever heard of something so ridiculous?"

The manager scowled at her, and explained, "For God's sake. *It's a knick-knack, Patty Whack, give the frog a loan! His old man's a Rolling Stone!*"

Portrait of an Artist

Feeling lonely, a big-city dweller named Throckmorton bought a parrot, brought it home, named it Wally. The next day, Throckmorton noticed that his new pet was using its claws to scratch drawings on the newspaper covering the bottom of the cage. Wally's drawings were not just the vagrant scratching of an ordinary bird. These doodles were incredibly vivid and evocative.

Throckmorton immediately ran out and bought some crayons for Polly. Using these tools, the parrot created shapes and colors of inarguable genius. For hours on end, Throckmorton would stay home and watch *Polly Wally doodle all day.*

Two Loopholes

In the late 1800s, not wanting to be outdone by American rodeo, an English chap decided to become a rodeo star. Not having a horse or any cattle, he cast about for some way to perform. His vocation was building outhouses, and he had several samples behind his home. He had also installed a couple of standing gas lamps in his yard. As a start, he decided that lassoing these objects would be good practice. After all, he reasoned, they may not be moving targets, but he could at least gain skill in controlling the rope.

Now he needed a mount. Not having a horse, he thought a bicycle would be a good substitute, and so he grabbed a coil of rope, hopped on his bicycle and off he went. He was phenomenally successful, and quickly got the hang of it. After the Englishman had been practicing for a couple of weeks, he could ride with no hands, twirling two lassoes at the same time. He proceeded to lasso an outhouse, then immediately followed with a perfect throw over one of the lamps, all the while singing, *"Here we go loop the loo. Here we go loop the light!"*

Ivy League

They were the first to attempt to colonize Mars. They knew it would be difficult, but they were determined to succeed.

They had landed with grass seeds to plant and embryos of horse, sheep, and cattle. But the grass wouldn't grow, and none of the calves survived. The horses and sheep were doing well, but there were not enough female animals to reproduce and meet their needs.

So they sent a message to earth asking for young female horses and sheep and a tasty, nutritious replacement for the grass. And they wanted an animal that could be used as meat in place of beef. Earth radioed back asking if venison would be satisfactory, and the colonists replied it would be.

A space shuttle arrived with the needed supplies. The bill of lading was rushed to the leader of the colony, who was delighted. "We got everything we asked for," he shouted. "They sent us *mare zygotes and doe zygotes and little lambs, sweet ivy.*"

A Zippy Game

Have you thought about acquiring the hot new educational video game for your kindergarten or first grader? Here's how it works:

The child is asked to point a laser beam at a letter of the alphabet that appears on a small ornamental thingamajig. Then, to solidify the child's learning, the player is asked to point the laser beam at an object on the screen that begins with the letter. Thus, if the child points the beam at the letter "A," he or she should then choose from among the pictures an apple.

If you wish your child to learn how to use the fourth letter in the alphabet by first pointing to the letter and then to the corresponding object, which in this case happens to be a district attorney, you would instruct the pupil, *"Zap a 'D' doodad; zap a D.A."*

The Last of the Red-Hot Lamas

The Dalai Lama had received permission from the Chinese government to restore a long unused Buddhist temple as a museum to extol the glories of the

People's Republic. The Lama felt that merely having access to the art and architectural treasures stored therein would help prevent the further loss of the Tibetan traditions.

As the Lama and his crew began clearing the temple, they were attacked by supernatural defenders of their faith, the Dakinis. Dakinis or "skywalkers," as they were commonly known, were ghostly women, of all sizes and skin colors, some with animal heads, each armed with a mystical weapon that could inflict severe physical damage on the living.

The crew refused to work, and the Lama called on Friar Harold Hillary, a famed exorcist, to help cleanse the abandoned temple of these unwanted spirits. Friar Harold rushed to the temple, armed with holy water and a nasty three-sided dagger called a "purba" that can pierce ghostly flesh. As the exorcist and the Lama entered the temple, a huge, lion-headed, dark green Dakini with a head-chopping sword gave an ear-shattering shriek. The exorcist splashed holy water on her, and she vanished. Then a giantess, at least twelve feet tall, a red-skinned Dakini, hurled an arm-binding noose over them, but the Friar stabbed her with the "purba," and she vanished. Next, a hugely obese Dakini, blue-black with flames shooting out of every pore, hurled a shoulder-piercing trident at the Lama, but he ducked and countered by chanting the weapon's mantra, "Phat!" and the monster vanished.

There were dozens of monsters, but the two vanquished every one. But one creature, of saffron hue and diminutive size, no bigger than a human thumb, managed to wound the exorcist in an embarrassing part of his anatomy. In his memoirs Fr. Harold described this skywalker: "She was *an itsy-bitsy, teeny-weeny, yellow poke-a-butt Dakini.*"

Pope and Circumstance

Joseph Alois Ratzinger was not the Cardinals' first choice for Pope. It was Cardinal Hans Grapje. Grapje was raised in a Catholic school and as a young man aspired to become a priest. However, he was drafted into the Army during World War II and spent two years co-piloting B17s until his aircraft was shot down in 1943, resulting in the loss of his left arm. Captain Grapje spent the rest of the war as a military chaplain, giving spiritual aid to soldiers, both Allied and enemy.

After the war, he became a priest, serving as a missionary in Africa, piloting his own plane (in spite of his handicap) to villages across the continent.

In 1997, Father Grapje (now an archbishop) was serving in Zimbabwe when an explosion in a silver mine caused a massive cave-in, trapping scores of miners deep in the earth. Archbishop Grapje went down into the mine to administer comfort and last rites to those too severely injured to move. Another shaft collapsed and entombed him for three days; he suffered multiple injuries, including the loss of his right eye.

Some time after being rescued, he developed a severe condition from his extensive underground exposure to the high silver content in the mine's air. It is characterized by purplish skin blotches and is found in many life-long silver miners.

For his heroism and selfless service to others, the church elevated him to Cardinal. With the passing of Pope John Paul II, he joined the other Cardinals in

Rome for the funeral and the conclave to select a new Pope from their ranks. Although Cardinal Grapje devoted his life to the service of God as a scholar, mentor, and holy man, church leaders felt that he could never ascend to the Papacy. The Church just couldn't accept *a one-eyed, one-armed, flying purple papal leader.*

Crowning Achievement

Fashions come and fashions go. When Queen Elizabeth II was coronated back in the late Fifties, women around the world flocked to buy those decorative jeweled headbands that look like small crowns and go with formal wear.

A leading fashion magazine blared a headline *TIARA BOOM TODAY!*

The Answers, My Friend

You Can Bank on It: "With a knick-knack, paddy whack. Give the dog a bone. This old man came rolling home" (*Knick-Knack Paddy Whack,* traditional)

Portrait of an Artist: "Polly wolly doodle all day" (*Polly Wolly Doodle,* traditional); *Two Loopholes:* "Here we go loop de loop Here we go loop de lie" (*Here we Go Loop De Loop,* traditional)

Ivy League: "Mairzy doats and dozy doats and liddle lamzy divey" (*Mairzy Doats* by Milton Drake, Al Hoffman, and Jerry Livingston)

A Zippy Game: "Zip-a-dee-doo-dah, zip-a-dee-ay" (*Zip-a-Dee-Doo-Dah,* by Allie Wrubel and Ray Gilbert, from the movie *Song of the South*)

The Last of the Red-Hot Lamas: "It was an itsy-bitsy, teenie-weenie, yellow polka-dot bikini" (*Itsy Bitsy, Teenie Weenie, Yellow Polka-Dot Bikini* by Paul Vance and Lee Pokriss)

Pope and Circumstance: "It was a one-eyed, one-horned, flyin' purple people eater" *(Purple People Eater* by Sheb Wooley)

Crowning Achievement: "Ta ra ra boom de ay" (*Ta Ra Ra Boom De Ay* by Henry J. Sayers; tune later adapted for the theme song of *The Howdy Doody Show*)

Chapter 9

Proud to be an American

The Spies of Life

During the most intensive days of the cold war, the Central Intelligence Agency undertook a recruitment drive to bolster its ranks and try to rectify the Soviet intelligence advantages. During the initial interviews, two candidates appeared particularly promising. Wayne and Amber were a brother and sister team. Although their fervor and patriotism could not be denied and their aptitude for spying was peerless, their one flaw was their inability to get along with each other.

Rarely did a moment go by when they weren't arguing, bickering, or insulting each other. As unorthodox as this behavior may have been, they were admitted to the CIA's training program and both excelled.

Their first assignment was to infiltrate a group of Soviet agents who were using Washington's night-clubs and restaurants as meeting places to plan their activities. Wayne and Amber had to become familiar with the coming and going of these restaurant patrons.

One night they had to visit five restaurants in a row. In order to protect their covers, they had to fit in with the restaurant crowd. That meant drinking and dining as legitimate patrons at these elegant eating establishments.

As they went from restaurant to restaurant, they argued, bickered, and screamed at each other, all the while eating full meals and drinking their fill. Because this was their first assignment, they were observed by a couple of CIA veterans. The observers were amazed by their huge appetites and their arguing. One observer turned to the other and said observantly, "They're *dutiful, voracious spies, but Amber raves at Wayne.*"

The Witching Time of Fright

There was a woman "of a certain age," and age had not been kind to her. In fact, her appearance caused some to call her a witch, a fact she eventually turned to her advantage. You see, the woman had seen both Hannibal Lecter movies and decided she would emulate his example. But unlike cannibal Hannibal, the woman ate only men and also wouldn't eat her victims raw. Instead, she cooked them, part by part, in her skillet.

When the police eventually arrested her, she

claimed, "I'm a witch. Cannibalism is part of my religion. You can't put me in jail for following my religion." Her defense partially succeeded, and instead of being sent to jail, she was banished from America.

She picked a faraway country to live in, hoping she could settle down unrecognized. Renouncing witchcraft, she joined a missionary church, led by a pastor named Pease, and became active in the church's chief activity. But despite her hope for a new life, unmarred by recognition of her former activities, she hadn't been living there long when she encountered a new neighbor who, on crossing paths with her, expressed displeasure at having her for a neighbor. Surprised, she asked, "Do you know who I am?"

The neighbor replied, *"You're a banned old hag, you're a guy-frying hag, and for Reverend Pease may you save."*

A Banner Day

When young José, newly arrived in the United States, made his first trip to Yankee Stadium, there were no tickets left for sale. Touched by his disappointment, a friendly ticket salesman found him a perch near the American flag. Later, José wrote home enthusiastically about his experience: "And the Americans, they are so friendly! Before the game started, they all stood up and looked at me and sang *'José, can you see?'*"

Doctor Do-A-Lot

Dr Doolittle's visage darkened as he dissected the diseased duodenum of the deceased male sheep. The good doctor declared that the malady was critically contagious and that it was our patriotic duty to guard the severed specimens from possible biological terrorists. So all through the night, *o'er the ram parts we watched*.

Old Soldiers

The general, ready to retire, decorated his new home to suit his tastes and the lifestyle he was about to adopt. Having lived a fully active life for so many years, he determined that henceforth he would live a life the opposite of what he had become used to — totally sedentary. He would recline away his days in splendor, on a freshly purchased bed with bedspread and sheets of vivid scarlet, where he would receive his three best buddies, generals who were retiring at the same time he was.

But of course, he had to make provisions for them to sit and relax in comfort when they visited him at "Columbia," as he called the house he'd purchased to retire in. What was the general's next purchase for this home? *Three chairs for the bed, bright and new.*

Stocking the Zoo

It is a little-known fact that the mother of famed game show host Monte Hall owned a company that provided exotic animals to zoos.

Equally little known is the fact that a few years ago, singer Dinah Shore was working to establish a zoo in the little Iowa town where she was born. It wasn't a very big zoo, but to give it a sense of substantialness, she named it after the widest shoe size that exists – Triple E. And Dinah, being a good family woman, employed great numbers of her relatives at the zoo.

As a long-time friend of Monte Hall, Dinah naturally bought many of the animals from his mother. In fact, many truckloads of animals were shipped from *the zoo of Monte Hall's ma to the Shores of Triple E!*

Hanky Panky

After her retirement from TV comedy, Sandy Duncan turned to drawing and painting in the small town she retired to. The townsfolk all heartily supported her budding talent and often asked the former comedienne to quickly sketch something for them on the spot. Sandy would smile broadly and grant their requests.

Soon her artistic talents were put to use on T-shirts, towels, and handkerchiefs – any cloth surface that would retain her eye-catching drawings.

On one steamy, hot Fourth of July, a little boy asked Ms. Duncan to create a drawing on a new, clean handkerchief. Full of artistic pride and the patriotic spirit of the day, she did so, softly singing to herself, "Oh, *I'm a hanky-doodling Sandy.*"

Perhaps you've already guessed what happened next. The little lad took his new treasure in his hand and proudly marched out the front door of the store loudly singing at the top of his lungs, *"I am a hanky-doodle boy!"*

Jest Ribbon You

Ty Cobb, after his illustrious baseball career, had a lot of trouble finding work. In desperation, he applied for a position as a chef at a retirement home, even though he was not trained as a chef. Throughout the interview, he was asked several times if he was really a master chef, and he lied each time, feeling more and more guilty about his cowardly deceit. In the end, however, he got the job.

The first day of work, he was assigned to make baked brie for his elderly clients. Not knowing a thing about cooking, he threw the cheese in the oven and left it there for two hours while he took a nap.

The cheese got all brown, burnt, and inedible, and Ty was awaked by the yelling manager, angrily pointing to the burned lump of cheese. "I thought you said you were a chef!" he shouted.

Ty began to stammer. "Oh! I lied sir, I lied! I was just so very scared of being broke and unemployed!"

"Well, look what your lies did!" stormed the manager angrily. *"Ty, your yellow fibbin' browned the old folks' brie!"*

Variety is the Very Spice

Famed British botanist Lord Ramsbottom successfully hybridized a cumin plant with a strain of coriander. The result was a cultivar that had a very unusual and highly desirable seed. The plant, when exhibited at local shows, won many awards. Lord Ramsbottom was so thrilled with his new hybrid that he showed the award-winning herb at the Royal Horticultural Society Exhibition at Kew Gardens in London.

One of the visitors to the exhibition was the owner of several greengrocer stores around London. His name was Abe Shapiro and he had found prosperity in England after emigrating from Minsk and working long and hard. Abe's knowledge of the market for herbs and spices was legendary and he was asked how he thought the newly developed strain would do in the marketplace.

He responded, "Vell, I t'ink it's a vunderful ting, dis new herb. So unusual. I can't belief dat *mine eyes haff seen the cory, and der cumin of da Lord."*

The Answers, My Friend

The Spies of Life: "Oh beautiful, for spacious skies, for amber waves of grain" (*America the Beautiful* by Samuel A. Ward and Katharine Lee Bates)

The Witching Time of Fright: "You're a grand old flag, you're a high-flying flag, and forever in peace may you wave" (*You're a Grand Old Flag* by George M. Cohan, from the stage musical *George Washington, Jr.*)

Banner Day: "Oh say can you see" (*The Star-Spangled Banner* by John Stafford Smith and Francis Scott Key)

Doctor Do-A-Lot: "O'er the ramparts we watched" (*The Star-Spangled Banner* by John Stafford Smith and Francis Scott Key)

Old Soldiers: "Three cheers for the red, white, and blue" (*Columbia, Gem of the Ocean* by T. Becket and D. Shaw)

Stocking the Zoo: "From the halls of Montezuma to the shores of Tripoli" (*The Marine Corps' Hymn,* music by Jacques Offenbach)

Hanky Panky "I'm a Yankee doodle dandy," "I'm that Yankee doodle boy" (*Yankee Doodle Dandy* by George M. Cohan, from the musical *Little Johnny Jones*)

Jest Ribbon You: "Tie a yellow ribbon round the ole oak tree" (*Tie a Yellow Ribbon Round the Ole Oak Tree* by L. Russell Brown and Irwin Levine)

Variety is the Very Spice: "Mine eyes have seen the glory of the coming of the Lord" (*Battle Hymn of the Republic by* Julia Ward Howe; same tune as *John Brown's Body*)

Chapter 10

That's All Folk

Weed It and Reap

Gloria, a constant gardener, had an industrial strength climbing rose. One day, the rosebush broke free from its trellis and started roaming through the rest of the flower bed, seeking other plants to devour. The nearest victim was a large and once promising herb, now starting to be engulfed by the rampant rose.

Fortunately, with clippers and twist tabs and lots of scratches, Gloria was able to untangle the rose, handcuff it back to the trellis, and salvage most of the battered herb.

She was very pleased to *partially save the rosemary in time.*

The Ant Farm

Old Jim Terwilliger did not appear to be much for words. Nor was he ever seen to have friends or pets. We thought he was the quintessential loner, until one time we caught him playing with his ant farm.

He loved the creatures. He knew more about ants than anyone knew about the streets in our little town, and he loved to talk about them. Indeed, it was a deep and private affair, and the townsfolk admired him for it.

One day tragedy hit in the form of a very high wind. It blew the top off the ant farm and his formicating pets were gone. With rivers of tears coursing down his cheeks, old Jim lamented, *"The ants are my friends. They're blowing in the wind. The ants they are blowing in the wind!"*

Stepping up to the Plate

At a party in the Hamptons one weekend given by the producer of a large network news show, one of the most famous of all on-camera personalities got something wedged in her "camera teeth." Being properly demure, she found her way to an upstairs bathroom, removed the teeth, and cleaned the offending "bit." Unfortunately, while re-inserting her pearly whites, she slipped on the tile floor. Her teeth flew out the window, clattered down the slate roof from the dormer, and lodged themselves in the gutter.

Most embarrassed, she went outside and explained to her host what had happened and asked if he had a ladder available.

"No need, ma'am, I've been experimenting with psychokinesis." He faced the roof and closed his eyes. Sure enough, the teeth rose up from the gutter, levitated across the intervening space, and landed in his hand.

A few minutes later, a hubbub arose when the neighbor's kitten, Amy, climbed a tree and immediately got stuck. Amidst shouts of "Call the Fire Department!" and "Call the SPCA," the producer said calmly, "That won't be necessary. *Like the bridge of our Barbara Walters, I will Amy down.*"

Just for the Halibut

Many landlubbers are unaware that the deep blue sea has a secret and highly developed social culture. There are many schools of thought as to its origins, and some feel it was developed eons ago when the Lost Continent of Atlantis was tragically sunk.

Our story concerns a carp rock group. The carp

who was the lead singer in the act was the owner of a very large and lovely bay, where he performed excellent songs of love. The mellifluous chords heard from his harp attracted schools and schools of grouper-ies, who tie-dyed their scales and pierced their gills, all trying to swim closer and closer to Carp and become his One True Love. They also admired his mussels. When he did his signature number "Harp-Sea-Chord," the crowd went wild!

An especially punked-out catfish named Bea swam to the concert one night, and our lead singing carp instantly became hooked on her. Objectively, Bea looked like a loose woman, with that hook sticking out of her bottom lip. Probably she'd been thrown back many a time by guys with all sorts of angles. But the carp loved her, and, moray to the point, he wanted her fin in marriage. But two things were floating in his way.

First, he was about to embark on a long ten-reefer tour in the SarGrasso Sea and was afraid that by the time he returned, Bea would have found another love. "Plenty of fish in the sea, Babe," she said. "I don't give a clam what you do."

Second, he really had nothing to offer Bea in the way of an engagement gift, since all he owned were his harp and his beautiful bay. He couldn't very well give her his harp, because then how would he go on tour?

So the carp made a decision. He would get a pre-Neptune-ual agreement and sign over his beautiful bay to her if she would only stay in it while he was gone, splashing around and cleaning stuff and doing his laundry with Tide. He approached Bea and sang to her this lovely song as his marriage proposal: *"If I*

were a Carp-On-Tour, though you ain't no lady,
would you marry me anyway and have my bay,
Bea?"

The Bear Facts

The off-his-rocker story writer and poet Edgar
Allan Poe developed a grudge against Smokey the
Bear (brother of Gladly, the Cross-Eyed Bear). Seems
that Poe loved the heat, look, and smell of blazes and
resented Smokey's long-time campaign to prevent
forest fires. So Poe sent a bunch of ravens to harass
Smokey by flying in circles around his head and caw-
ing raucously. This drove Smokey to distraction, but
he was too old and weak to ward off the marauding
birds.

Well, I'm a big fan of Smokey and his campaign to
keep our forests safe. So when word of his plight
reached me, I immediately set out to help him with
the aid of my loyal dog, Rover. You see, Rover was a
bird dog, and his breed specialized in getting rid of
pesky ravens.

As soon as Rover and I arrived on the scene, we
sprang into action. Rover jumped into my arms, and I
threw him up high, toward Smokey's head. My little
dog snarled and barked loudly, scaring away the
black birds. I then wrote Edgar Allan a letter describ-
ing what had happened: *"On top of Old Smokey, all*
covered with crows, I tossed my true Rover, thus
thwarting you, Poe."

Ex Post Fact

Emily Post is considered to have written the finest
books on etiquette in history. Her name has become
synonymous with proper behavior throughout soci-

ety and is still the primary reference for planning social events.

One day, a group of club women called Emily and asked her to attend their gala event to accept their prestigious award for her contributions to living the more civilized and courteous life. When she received her award at the ceremonies, Ms. Post humbly explained, "Aw shucks. *It's nothing but a fine couth tome.*"

Cock of the Walk

Rudy the Rooster ruled the roost. Because he was in such great shape, all the other roosters on the chicken farm feared him. His shapely body also made him a ladies' bird, and he could swoop around the coop and connect with any hen he wished.

Rudy had a strange way of maintaining his body beautiful. He would sandpaper his biceps to sculpt them in shapes attractive to the opposite sex and fear-inspiring to other males. On some days you could hear Rudy scraping away till late in the afternoon. It just goes to show that, to remain an alpha bird, a *flying cock'll sand muscles till five in the day.*

The Answers, My Friend

The Ant Farm: "The answer, my friends, is blowing in the wind. The answer is blowing in the wind" (*Blowin' in the Wind* by Bob Dylan)

Stepping up to the Plate: "Like a bridge over troubled water, I will lay me down" (*Bridge over Troubled Water* by Paul Simon)

Weed it and Reap: "Parsley, sage, rosemary, and thyme" (*Scarborough Fair,* traditional)

Just for the Halibut: "If I were a carpenter, and you were a lady, would you marry me anyway? Would you have my baby?" (*If I Were a Carpenter* by Tim Hardin)

The Bear Facts: "On top of Old Smokey, all covered with snow, I lost my true lover for courtin' too slow" (*On Top of Old Smokey,* traditional song)

Ex Post Fact: "With nothing but a fine tooth comb" (*Bill Bailey* by Hughie Cannon)

Cock of the Walk: "Crying, 'cockles and mussels, alive alive oh'" (*Molly Malone* by James Yorkston)

Chapter 11

Have a Punny Christmas

A Full Plate

A man went to his dentist because he felt some-thing wrong in his mouth. The dentist looked in-side and said, "That new upper plate I put in for you six months ago is eroding. What have you been eat-ing?"

The man replied, "All I can think of is that about four months ago my wife made some asparagus and put some Hollandaise sauce on it. I loved it so much I now put it on everything — meat, toast, fish, vegeta-bles, everything!"

"Well," said the dentist, "that's probably the problem. Hollandaise sauce is made with lots of lemon juice, which is highly corrosive. It's eaten away your upper plate. I'll make you a new plate, and this time use chrome."

"Why chrome?" asked the patient.

"It's simple," replied the dentist. "Dental researchers have concluded that *there's no plate like chrome for the Hollandaise!*"

Chinks in the Armor

Sir Granville knew he faced a fierce battle from the invading Celtic hoards. He felt he could defeat the invaders even though his forces had been weakened by previous battles.

He sent his page to his closest neighboring lord, Sir Simon, and requested assistance. Fearing an invasion of his own territory, Simon sent back only one of his knights to help Granville during the coming battle.

The expected battle ensued, and Sir Granville's forces were virtually unharmed. There was only one major casualty, the knight sent by Simon who, though alive, had received multiple sword wounds to his chest and abdomen.

The page was sent from battle to notify his lord of the results. He happily reported the success, but was saddened to report, *"Sy's lent knight's a holey knight."*

Weather or Not

Rudolph, a dedicated Russian Communist, was the most famous weather man in Russia. That was because he always predicted the weather with 100 percent accuracy.

Rudolph was called to a rocket base by the government because they were about to launch a large satellite. He looked at the sky and urged the scientists and engineers to postpone the launch because, he asserted, a hard rain would soon fall.

Rudolph's wife, who happened to be the chief scientist at the launch site, urged Rudolph to change his mind and give his go-ahead to the launch. She argued that there wasn't a cloud anywhere within ten miles of the base. As a matter of fact, that day had been the most beautiful day in months, and it was obvious to everyone that it wasn't going to rain.

Their collegial disagreement soon escalated into a furious argument that Rudolph closed by shouting, *"Rudolph the Red knows rain, dear!"*

Doe, a Deer

The game show contestant was only 200 points behind the leader and about to answer the final question, worth 500 points!

"To be today's champion," the show's smiling host intoned, "name two of Santa's reindeer."

The contestant, a man in his early thirties, gave a sigh of relief, gratified that he had drawn such an easy question.

"Rudolph!" he said confidently, "and . . .Olive!"

The studio audience started to applaud (like the little sign above their heads said to do,) but the clapping quickly faded into mumbling, and the confused host replied, "Yes, we'll accept Rudolph, but could you please explain Olive?"

"You know," the man circled his hand forward impatiently and began to sing, "Rudolph the Red Nosed

Reindeer had a very shiny nose. And if you ever saw it, you would even say it glowed. *Olive, the other reindeer . . . ."*

Check, Mate.

A group of chess-playing fanatics would gather each morning in the hotel lobby to brag about their greatest victories. It seemed that each player had only triumphs and awesome feats of skill to his credit. Finally the hotel manager barred the group from the lobby, because he couldn't stand to hear a bunch of *chess nuts boasting in an open foyer.*

Wig Deal

Three aged angels in retirement found that their cash was starting to run out. The trio desperately needed money, not only to acquire basic necessities, but to buy bright jewelry for themselves to add to their luminescence.

So they went to a financial adviser. She looked them over and noted that, although the three angels had become wrinkled, they still sported gorgeous heads of golden locks and tresses.

Realizing that such spectacular hair would be in great demand from wigmakers, the adviser advised the trio to *"hock the hair, old angels. Bring glory and some new-earned bling."*

Notion for a Lotion

A Christmas tree salesman usually vacationed in sunny Florida right after he closed his lot, and always suffered a painful sunburn until he started producing a suntan lotion made from his unsold trees. The pine-scented lotion was called, *"O Tannin' Balm."*

Up a Tree

A mother was pleased with the card her son had made her for Christmas, but was puzzled as to the scraggly-looking tree from which many presents dangled, and near the top, something that looked strangely like a bullet. She asked him if he would explain the drawing and why the tree itself was so bare, instead of a fat pine tree. "It's not a traditional Christmas tree," he explained. "It's *a cartridge in a bare tree.*"

Fan Dumb

One of rock and roll's earliest and greatest performers was the incomparable Buddy Holly. Despite his bespectacled, nerdy appearance, the man really knew how to ignite an audience. In fact, the folks who attended Buddy's performances got so excited that many of his concerts ended with a riot. Just as soon as the fans saw that Buddy had performed the closing song, they would fly into a collective rage, smash chairs, storm the stage, and tear down the curtain. So no theater owner would hire Buddy because they feared that their patrons would *wreck the halls, with bows of Holly.*

Going Ape

A zoo featured a spacious gorilla exhibition. The caged area was huge and filled with sturdy playground equipment, including a tire on a rope, a sliding board, and a jungle gym. The gorillas moved freely from one apparatus to another, which encouraged their natural instincts to assert themselves.

Two of the apes especially loved a barrel that had been provided. They would make a beeline – an apeline, actually – for that piece of equipment, and one of them would toss it over his head and wear it around his considerable waist. You could almost hear them exult, *"Don we now our play ape barrel!"*

The Christmas Dinner

Grandpa and grandma were planning to host the annual family Christmas dinner. About forty guests were expected, and they spent a full week in preparations. As the big day approached, grandpa got into his car to make one last run to the grocery store.

As grandpa started pulling away, their daughter, Debbie, came running out the door shouting frantically, "Stop! Mom says wait! *She's making a list. She's checking it twice. She says she needs some chicken and rice."*

Drama King

The author of *Who's Afraid of Virginia Wolfe* left the theater on a cold and foggy winter night prepared to sing a song of tribute to the weather. Alas, he had forgotten the words of the song and had to just hum the melody. A husband walking by asked his wife, "What's he doing?"

She answered, *"Albee hums for crisp mist."*

Tarnation

Three circus midgets decided to change professions. They reviewed their options and decided to move to China and start a business together in that burgeoning economy. They bought a factory in Beijing and started manufacturing road-building materials to use to build highways for China's expanding transportation system. They shrewdly cornered the market on a black, sticky substance to cover the roads they were building. Thus, they became known as the *three wee kings of Orient tar.*

The Answers, My Friend

A Full Plate: "There's no place like home for the holidays" (*Home for the Holidays* by Robert Allen and Al Stillman)

Chinks in the Armor: "Silent night, holy night" (*Silent Night* by Franz X. Gruber and Josef Mohr)

Weather or Not: "Rudolph the red-nosed reindeer" (*Rudolph the Red-Nosed Reindeer* by Johnny Marks)

Doe, a Deer: "All of the other reindeer" *(Rudolph the Red-Nosed Reindeer)*

Check, Mate: "Chestnuts roasting on an open fire" (*The Christmas Song* by Robert Wells and Mel Torme)

Wig Deal: Hark! The herald angels sing. Glory to our new-born king" (*Hark! The Herald Angels Sing* by Felix Mendelssohn and Charles Wesley)

Notion for a Lotion: "O Tannenbaum" (*O Tannenbaum* by Ernst Anschutz)

Fan Dumb: Deck the halls with bows of holly (*Deck the Hall,* traditional)

Going Ape: Don we now our gay apparel *(Deck the Hall,* traditional)

The Christmas Dinner: "He's making a list. He's checking it twice. He's going to find out who's naughty or nice" (*Santa Claus Is Coming to Town* by J. Fred Coots and Haven Gillespie)

Drama King: "I'll be home for Christmas" (*I'll Be Home for Christmas* by Kim Gannon and Walter Kent)

Up a Tree: "A partridge in a pear tree" *(The Twelve Days of Christmas,* traditional)

Tarnation: "We three kings of Orient are" (*We Three Kings* by John Henry Hopkins, Jr.)

Chapter 12

Give Me That Old Time Religion

A Wrenching Experience

There was once a handyman who had a dog named Mace. Mace was a great dog, except he had one weird habit: He liked to eat grass — not just a little bit, but in quantities that would make a lawnmower blush. And nothing, it seemed, could cure him of it.

One day, the handyman lost his wrench in the tall grass while he was working outside. He looked and looked, but it was nowhere to be found. As it was getting dark, he gave up for the night and decided to look the next morning.

When he awoke, he went outside, and saw that his dog had eaten the grass, around where he had been working, and his wrench now lay in plain sight, glinting in the sun. Going out to get his wrench, the handyman called the dog over to him and said, *"A'grazing Mace, how sweet the hound that saved a wrench for me."*

Commercial Success

A certain artificial sweetener company wanted to spruce up its image with a big new ad campaign. The marketing department quickly divided into two squabbling factions. One group wanted to do a "Big Band Nostalgia" theme, sponsoring some jazzy, happenin' musical events, while the other group was dead set on a tribute to the classic movie *Ben-Hur*, complete with a real live reenactment of the iconic chariot race.

As the deadline approached, no one would budge, so finally the two sides were forced to compromise. When the big boss came to see the finished product, he was presented with a snappy jazzy orchestra seated in a giant Roman vehicle. "What is that?" he cried.

"Well sir," replied his v.p. of marketing, "That is the *Sweet & Low swing chariot!"*

Scroll Call

Archeology, that ancient science of antiquities (or is it the antiquated science of ancients?), received much favorable press with the Indiana Jones sagas.

Usually, though, archeology is more quiet than that.

One exception to this quiet occurred a few years ago in the Middle East when a new cache of ancient written material was found near the Northern border of the Dead Sea. Controversy arose immediately. It appeared that while many of the documents were authentic, several were much more recent forgeries.

What a potential calamity! The archeologists, who all lived much farther to the South, argued about what to do. It was decided that by combining their expertise, they would be able to discard the bogus material. In fact, each one of them was heard to agree that, *"When the scrolls are culled up yonder, I'll be there!"*

Walking the Walk

"So," asked the teacher, "what are the names used for the Supreme Being and the great religious leaders?"

The names came rattling out – "God," "Lord," "Yahweh," "Jehovah," "King," "Creator," "Maker," and so forth.

Little Johnny remained silent. "So Johnny, can *you* think of any?"

He scratched his head, then said, "Art, Harold, and Andy!"

"Art, Harold, and Andy? The Supreme Being?"

"Oh, yes. You know, there's the prayer 'Our Father, Art, in heaven, Harold be thy name.' And I just heard a hymn: *'Andy walks with me, Andy talks with me!'* "

Puckish Humor

A father and son were rabid fans of the Boston Bruins. They had season tickets and never missed a home game. Their seats were as close as possible to their favorite player – the Bruins goalie. Each game they would lustily cheer his exploits.

After several seasons, the goalie started skating over to the father's and son's seats after a game to chat. Soon the three struck up a friendship, and the goalie invited the father and son to his home for dinner. The pro piled the table with delicious food, including some bread that he had baked from his own recipe. It was called *Hockey Mountain Rye*.

A sportswriter got wind of this family story and wrote a warm and fuzzy column about it. He told how wonderful relationships like these were for professional sports and managed to effusively *praise father, son, and goalie host*.

A Finny Line

Many a fund-raising campaign has been launched to assist the starving in India where famine, like death and taxes, seems inevitable. There is an apocryphal story about the illustrious Joey Smallwood, premier of Newfoundland. Touched by the plight of the East Indian, he sent a large portion of the annual seafood catch from the Grand Banks. When the fish had been loaded aboard the mercy freighter, the captain thought some historic message should accompany the generous gift. He radioed Smallwood, asking if he would apply his ingenuity to the idea. The premier was equal to the demand. He wirelessed back: *"Nehru, my cod to thee."*

A Grizzly Situation

As all college sports fans know, in Texas they play *serious* football. Even the mascots are generally serious. In Houston, they have a cougar. At Texas, they have a longhorn steer. And at Baylor they have a bear.

This story is about one of the recent Baylor mascots. Now, you have to remember that Baylor University (aka Jerusalem on the Brazos) is a Baptist university. They try very seriously to bring this affiliation into all aspects of university life — including the mascot.

It is sad to have to tell this, but the recent mascot was a visually challenged member of the ursine species. His right eye looked to the left, and his left eye looked to the right. In all other respects, he was an exemplary creature, so the university decided to put up with the defect. In fact, in keeping with their religious affiliation, they decided to name the animal "Gladly." As in *Gladly, the cross-eyed bear.*

Time for Anger

Herman was afflicted with an explosive personality that caused him more and more problems at home and on the job. Finally, his distressed family persuaded him to enter an anger-management course.

Herman's therapy included an alarm clock on his bedroom table that was tuned in to his brain by electronic pulses. Every time Herman flew into a tantrum, the clock would explode into a loud and irritating ring that wouldn't stop until he calmed down. For quite a while, Herman deeply resented the noisy timepiece, but eventually he came to see that it was helping him to control his anger. He would even sing to it: *"Clock of rages, left for me. Let me chide myself with thee."*

Sticky Business

While sorting and counting the money from the church's collection plate, the new deacon noticed that many of the bills were sticking together. At first he thought some careless child with dirty fingers had inadvertently polluted the currency with the residue of a sweet snack.

Oddly enough there wasn't really anything obviously sticky. Many of the dollars were merely clinging together tightly as if held by magnetism. It was quite a task to pry them apart without ripping them. He shared this curious fact with the minister, who calmly reassured him that this was not at all uncommon. *"These are the tithes that bind,"* he noted.

A Sonnet

A man named Noah Williamson, in days
before refrigerators, had to go
on a long trip and simply did not know
some of the more sophisticated ways
to preserve food. As was often the case
with traders, through his house would often flow
barrels of goods. He did not wish to throw
them all away, so he crushed ice to stay
deterioration, and put some inside
each barrel. On returning home, did he
open the lard, and right away he spied
an oily coating, and could plainly see
the ice was dirty, though it was still hard.
Noah found grease in the ice of the lard!

The Answers, My Friend

A Wrenching Experience: "Amazing grace, how sweet the sound that saved a wretch like me" (*Amazing Grace* by John Newton)

Commercial Success: "Swing low, sweet chariot" (*Swing Low, Sweet Chariot,* traditional)

Scroll Call: "When the role is called up yonder, I'll be there" (*When the Role Is Called Up Yonder* by James M. Black)

Walking the Walk: "And He walks with me, and He talks with me" (*In the Garden* by C. Austin Miles)

Puckish Humor: "Praise Father, Son, and Holy Ghost" (*Glory to Thee, My God, Tonight* by Thomas Tallis and Thomas Ken)

Finny Line: "Nearer, my God, to Thee" (*Nearer, My God, to Thee* by Lowell Mason and Sarah Adams)

A Grizzly Situation: "Gladly the cross I'd bear" (*Keep Thou My Way* by Francis Crosby)

Time for Anger: "Rock of ages, cleft for me. Let me hide myself in thee" (*Rock of Ages* by Thomas Hastings and Augustus M. Topland)

Sticky Business: "Blest be the ties that bind" (*Blest Be the Tie That Binds* by John Fawcett)

A Sonnet: "Noah found grace in the eyes of the Lord" (*Noah Found Grace in the Eyes of the Lord,* traditional)

Chapter 13

Go Western, Young Man

The Lone Arranger

In a ranch kitchen sat a wood range for cooking and, as well, a second, older stove, rusting and decrepit, no longer useful except as a table. On top of the second appliance was a squat refrigerator to keep the melon and milk cool during the hot summer. It also held some beer.

The door opened and in came Cactus, one of the hands. He reached into the old refrigerator for a beer and held it down on the top to uncap it. The froth bubbled up and flowed down the cold bottle, and from there it dripped on to the old stove. The mess that resulted was *foam, foam on the range, where the beer and the cantaloupe stay.*

Statue of Imitations

Martha Martin was the sculptor in charge of making the Oscars for each annual presentation of the Academy Awards. One day she got fired and a replacement was brought in, but the resulting statuettes were all cracked or misshapen or dull in finish.

In desperation, the powers that be rehired Martha and asked her why her Oscar statues always turned out perfect, while those of her successor were disasters. She explained, *"You gotta know when to mold 'em and know when to gold 'em."*

You'll Get a Kick out of This

There was once a herd of llamas that lived next to a herd of cows, separated only by a small fence. The cows would trick the young llamas into coming near the fence. When the small llamas got close enough, the bovines would grab them and pull them over to their side. Then they'd kick the llamas around, using them like soccer balls.

The moral of the story: *Llamas, don't let your babies grow up to be cow toys.*

Dear Cabbie

George W. Bush arrived at the Dallas airport and had to get to an important meeting. His limo wasn't there to pick him up, so he was forced to select a cab from the groups parked in front of the terminal. It was the first time in a long while that he had seen *the yellow rows of taxis.*

And ever since, President Bush's chief of staff has made sure that a similar row of taxis greets the President at every airport. Mr. Bush has come to see that an important part of his *life is a cab array.*

Gag Time

Young José Hernandez was wanted by the police, but before his youthful, illegal indiscretions, his history is a most fascinating one. José was the illegitimate son of a nun, and he was raised in a convent in northeastern Spain, near Barcelona.

Among the skills he learned while growing up were flute and horn playing. Eventually he left the convent and became a musician of minor celebrity in the Barcelona area. However, as a flute player, gigs were infrequent.

Eventually "Joe" Hernandez escaped his low-paying musician's job in Spain and traveled to the Middle East, trying to eke out a living. But wages were either low or non-existent for a nun's son whose only skill was flute and horn playing.

Joe tried farming, but never adjusted to rural life. After working as a part-time farmer and pushing a plow, he quit that job. Finding himself destitute in Israel, Joe was forced into a life of crime. He robbed a museum in the city of Haifa, Israel, and got away with many of the city of Haifa's historical relics.

The people were upset that their historical and religious icons had been pilfered. The Israeli police put out an all-points bulletin asking citizens to be on the lookout for *a Haifa-lootin', flutin', tootin' son of a nun from Barcelona, part-time plowboy Joe.*

Bad to Verse

The wild and wooly west was replete with adventure and potential riches. Magical artifacts were reputed to be abundant and highly sought after. One little town, La Poema, near the Superstition Mountains, became famous for a particular enchanted pebble that was available for viewing in the public library.

The locals particularly appreciated the sight of strangers touching the stone and uncontrollably bursting into verse. For example, a hardtack miner spouted, "Dagnabit, this mangy rabbit, has a bad habit" before he was able to pull his hand away. An elderly spinster was heard to say, "While playing scrabble, with the local rabble, who like to gabble, I like to dabble . . ." — and then she jerked her hand back before getting even more in trouble. A child with consumption touched the pebble and complained, "Ruin and wrack, spew and hack. Alas, alack. True health I lack, I'm going back, to . . ." before he was dragged away.

One cowhand observer knew better than to touch the stone. However, his curiosity made him ask the locals, "What is that pebble that makes these people spout all those words that sound so much alike?" The only possible answer came back, *"It's a rhyme stone, cowboy."*

Playboy of the Western World

When Hugh Hefner had his Playboy mansion, there were a succession of Playboy bunnies that he became involved with. It was a custom for each bunny to present him with a necktie. Eventually, he had hundreds of them in his closet.

When he finally married Kimberly Conrad, she became upset to see all those souvenirs from former girlfriends. In a fit of pique, she grabbed them all and threw them at her new husband, which led to the famous song, *"The ties of exes are upon Hugh."*

The Write Way

An aspiring author set out to write the great American novel, but, over the years, his manuscripts were unfailingly rejected. Worse, editors usually affixed notes telling him that his writing was clunky and his storylines boring.

Needing to make a living, the author became what's known in the trade as a "book doctor," improving the manuscripts of other authors. He was so good at making better the works of others that he commanded handsome fees, even though he himself never received credit for his contributions. His friends said to each other, "We always knew there was a *ghost writer in this guy."*

Miss Soldier of Fortune

One of the more interesting love stories to come out of Tinseltown was that of the brief but torrid romance between Sylvester Stallone and a comely young lady named Lynne Rose Murphy. He met her at a convention sponsored by *Soldier of Fortune* magazine at which he was a judge. She was a contestant vying for the title of "Miss Soldier of Fortune."

She won the contest in a runaway after demonstrating her prowess in the martial arts, including hand-to-hand and weapons combat. Smitten by her abilities and physical strength, Stallone said, "She is definitely *my Rambo Lynne Rose."*

Double Double, Toilet Trouble

A plumber purchased a seal pup from a marine animal rescue service. He brought the slippery little fellow up to be his valued assistant on the job. As the seal matured, it became a specialist in fixing toilet problems. The flippered creature could balance its tools on its nose while repairing a flush mechanism, reversing an overflow in the toilet bowl, and fixing dozens of other toilet problems. And the novelty of a seal plumber caused business to boom.

But one day, the seal got the urge to join the circus. The animal was such a quick study that it became a star overnight, balancing balls upon its nose and playing complicated musical compositions on a row of horns.

Lamented the bereft plumber, *"You picked a fine time to leave me, loo seal!"*

Clowning Around

When country singer Crystal Gayle was a little girl, she had a passion for clown dolls. But her family didn't have a lot of money for such luxuries, so her very talented mom devoted long evenings by the fire hand crafting beautiful and interesting harlequin dolls for her daughter.

Once, while creating a particularly special and intricately designed doll, Momma ran into a problem. The tiny blue faux crystals that she had chosen for the eyes simply would not stay put no matter what kind of adhesive she tried.

Fretting, she asked her little girl to run out and buy some especially sticky Krispy Kremes. Perhaps those would attach those pesky little gems to the clown's face.

Well, believe it or not, it worked. Little Crystal exclaimed, "Oh, Momma, look! *Donuts make my clown eyes glue.*"

Space Opera

It's a long, long time from now, and machines have developed into sentient beings. Starting with the high-tech space stuff, a whole new set of different mechanistic species have come into existence. The machines are not only sentient; they are alive in other ways as well. They even produce offspring and evolve.

At first, it was just the super high-tech orbiting stuff that achieved self-awareness, but soon more terrestrial devices gained intelligence. Unfortunately the machines loathed each other, and war broke out between orbiting and earthly devices. Humankind had already moved out into space, but at the discovery that our original home world was in a crisis situation, we returned.

By the time we reached Earth again, all the original machines had been destroyed. The descendants of those original devices were still battling, trying to obliterate each other — an ancient blood feud where one planetary region wasn't big enough for the two mechanical clans.

The future humans had to make a decision that would end the war. But it was clear that humankind had been in space too long as there was no sympathy for the terrestrial machines. And that's when we found ourselves *backing the satellite kin.*

A Sonnet

A chef invented a brand new dessert —
chocolate mousse on a stick — but in his haste,
alas, I am afraid it ne'er occurred
to him the stick might clash with the great taste.
He sought to change this, and so on a trial
basis he made a syrup that would meet
his needs. He placed a spoonful in a vial,
and left the stick in till it tasted sweet.
The first ones were too sweet, and this was not
desirable. In time he's toned it down —
the sugar, so the last are mild. He's got
vials from when he started, and won't frown
at a request for sweetness. His answer's quick:
*"The older the vial it's in, the sweeter the mousse
stick!"*

The Answers, My Friend

The Lone Arranger: "Home, home on the range, where the deer and the antelope play" (*Home on the Range* by Dan Kelly and Brewster Higley)

Statue of Imitations: "You gotta know when to hold 'em and know when to fold 'em" (*The Gambler* by Don Schlitz)

You'll Get a Kick out of This: "Mammas, don't let your babies grow up to be cowboys" (*Mammas, Don't Let Your Babies Grow Up to Be Cowboys* by Ed Bruce and Patsy Bruce)

Dear Cabbie: "The yellow rose of Texas" (*The Yellow Rose of Texas* by Jay Livingston and Ray Evans, from the movie *Captain Carey, USA*); "Life is a cabaret" (*Cabaret,* from *Cabaret* by John Kander and Fred Ebb)

Gag Time: "A rootin'- tootin' high falutin' son of a gun from Arizona, ragtime cowboy Joe (*Ragtime Cowboy Joe,* by Maurice Abrahams, Lewis F. Muir, and Grant Clarke)

Bad to Verse: "He's a rhinestone cowboy" (*Rhinestone Cowboy* by Larry Weiss);

Playboy of the Western World: "The eyes of Texas are upon you" (*The Eyes of Texas* by John Sinclair; same tune as *I've Been Working on the Railroad)*

The Write Way: "The ghost riders in the sky" (*[Ghost] Riders in the Sky* by Stan Jones)

Miss Soldier of Fortune: "My ramblin' rose" (*Ramblin' Rose* by Noel Sherman and Joe Sherman)

Clowning Around: Don't it make my brown eyes blue" (*Don't It Make My Brown Eyes Blue* by Richard Leigh)

Double Double, Toilet Trouble; "You picked a fine time to leave me, Lucille" (*Lucille* by Roger Bowling and Ray Whitley);

Space Opera: "Back in the saddle again" (*Back in the Saddle Again* by Ray Whitley, from the film *Border G-Men;* later the theme song for Gene Autrey

A Sonnet: "The older the violin, the sweeter the music" (*The Older the Violin, the Sweeter the Music* by Curly Putman)

Chapter 14

Code of Ethics

The Server Is Down

The fairy Tinker Bell hoped to be Peter Pan's companion, but he rejected her for the more mundane Wendy. Devastated by this downturn of events, Tinker Bell decided to get as far away from Never-Never Land as she could. Her flight from fantasy land ended in Fresno, California, where she became a waitress at a roadside truckstop.

One day an especially rowdy group of truckers came into the restaurant. They got roaring drunk, spoke loudly and rudely, slopped chunks of food all over the table and floor, and left Tinker Bell a measly quarter gratuity per trucker. The enraged sprite literally flew into a tantrum, pointed to one of the paltry coins, and screamed, *"It's the wrong way to tip a fairy, who's a long way from home!"*

Spies Spied

During World War II, the captured Allied agents of Stalag 15 were attempting yet another daring prison break. On this particular night, Major O'Roarke and Lieutenant Flanagan were chosen to try to cut their way out of the east gate. They were hard at work when the siren sounded, and the floodlights caught them in the act.

As the German officer led them away, O'Roarke asked, "We were so careful. How did you catch us?"

The German replied, "It's very simple. Somehow, I can always tell *when Irish spies are filing."*

Accidents Happen

Seamus fell off a tractor belonging to his neighbor, Colin O'Toole, banging his leg on a manifold sticking out of the side of the engine. When Seamus's son asked him where it hurt, Seamus moaned in agony, *"Ohhh! Da knee, boy! The pipes, the pipes o' Colin."*

Donkey Hotay

An Irishman named O'Leary, who loved to sing as he worked, bought a mule to farm his garden. The mule worked well but was almost totally deaf. So, when his owner yelled, "Whoa!" the animal often continued plowing.

Asked how the mule was working out, O'Leary

shook his head in resignation. "There was a time," he said, "when all the neighbors could hear was me singing my lilting melodies. But lately, I'm afraid, they've heard nothing but *my riled Irish whoa's!*"

Killarney Blarney

In Florida, a group started a con ring that went to old-folks homes and offered trips to the homeland, Ireland. After securing their down payment (usually around a thousand dollars), the con artists would split. When the scam was discovered, the story ran in the local papers under the headline *TOUR ALLURE A LIE.*

Tilde Cows Come Home

The "~" thing in Spanish has a name — the "tilde." Walt Disney often used Spanish themes in his films and, as a result, became one of the most avid advocates of the tilde. Indeed, until his death, he devoted untold hours making others aware of its potential.

So today, whenever I use that little button on the upper left of my computer keyboard, I often feel like *Walt's in my tilde.*

Smell Me a River

An old industrial town decided it was time to clean up the local waterway. Engineers built a series of diversionary trenches to capture some of the solid pollutants. Unfortunately, the vastly increased concentration of pollutants in these trenches caused a greatly obnoxious odor in the neighborhood, prompting locals to lament the presence of *a river ditch aroma.*

Leapin' Lizards!

The Israelis created a new drink in which they mixed the ingredients of an egg cream (long a popular Jewish treat) with the body of a Gila monster. That might strike you as bizarre, but – hey! – Israelis live in the desert, and somebody had to find some way to use those lizards to create a new taste sensation. So now, one Israeli is often heard to say to another, *"Have an egg Gila."*

A Chat about a Choo Choo

It was my first tour into outer space, and we were scheduled to spend two weeks on the satellite. Just before leaving, as I hugged my wife and children goodbye, my four-year-old son, Bobbie, handed me his stuffed choo-choo engine and told me, "Take this, Daddy. It will bring you good luck."

The mission was a success and as we were getting ready to return to Earth, I realized I'd forgotten to pack Bobbie's choo-choo. I rushed back to the sleeping quarters and picked it up, but as I was getting into the return ship, it slipped out of my hands. I wanted to retrieve it, but there was no time and it had to be left behind.

When I was reunited joyfully with my family, and after all the hugs and kisses, Bobbie asked me, "Where is my choo choo?" I told him, "I am sorry, but *by Mir is your train.*"

Sign Language

There is a little village in Wales named: "LAN-FAIRPWLLGWYNGYLLGOGERYCHWYRNDROBWLL-LLANTYSILIOGOGOGOC." Many, many years ago, on the side of the road leading into the village, there was a sign announcing the town's name, made of letters carved in wood. Naturally this sign was very long and very expensive to maintain.

One day, the village council, always short of money, decided to replace the long wooden sign with a short metal sign which wouldn't cost so much to maintain. They decided to offer the old sign to any museum that was interested. The Scottish National Museum offered to take the sign and display it. Robert Burns saw it and was so impressed he wrote the now-famous Scottish song, *"Old Long Sign."*

An In-Tents Adventure

A man started a tradition of taking his young son camping every New Year's Eve. Although they lived in the South, it still got cold on New Year's Eve, but it was not the biting cold of the North. With the older man and the young fellow bundled up warmly, the temperatures were not unbearable. But the son didn't have the taste for camping and for nature that his dad did.

Their equipment was on the primitive side: They slept in plain old sleeping bags inside an old World War I army surplus tent.

Alas, one year the well-worn tent finally succumbed to a rip in the canvas, and in the middle of the night a nocturnal bird got into the tent, startling the son. Frightened, he grabbed up his backpack and sleeping bag, pulled his dad to his feet, and headed out into the night, running toward where they had left their van.

"Wait!" said the father, mindful that the son was leaving something behind. *"Should owled and quaint tents be forgot?"*

The Answers, My Friend

The Server Is Down: "It's a long way to Tipperary. It's a long way to go" *(It's a Long Way to Tipperary* by Jack Judge and Harry Williams*)*

Spies Spied: "When Irish eyes are smiling" (*When Irish Eyes Are Smiling* by Ernest Ball, Chauncey Olcott, and George Graff, Jr.)

Accidents Happen: "Oh Danny boy, the pipes, the pipes are calling (*Londonderry Air,* by Frederick Edward Weatherly)

Donkey Hotay: "My wild Irish rose" (*My Wild Irish Rose* by Chancellor "Chancey" Olcott)

Killarney Blarney: "Too-ra-loo-ra-loo-ra" (*Too-Ra-Loo-Ra-Loo-Ra;* by James Royce Shannon)

Tilde Cows Come Home: "Waltzing Matilda" (*Waltzing Matilda* by Banjo Paterson)

Smell Me a River: "Arrivederchi, Roma" (*Arrivederchi, Roma* by Renatto Ranucci and Carl Sigman)

My Little Dumpling: "'Twas on the Isle of Capri that I found her" (*Isle of Capri* by Will Gross and Jimmy Kennedy)

Ember Alert: "Danke schoen" (*Danke Schoen* by Bert Kaempfert, Kurt Schwaback, and Milt Gabler)

Leapin' Lizards!: "Havah nagilah" (*Havah Nagilah,* traditional)

A Chat about a Choo-Choo: "Bei mir bist du schoen" (*Bei Mir Bis Du Schoen,* from the musical *I Would If I Could* by Sholom Secunda and Jacob Jacobs)

Sign Language: "Auld Lang Syne" (*Auld Lang Syne* by Robert Burns)

An In-Tents Adventure: "Should auld acquaintance be forgot" *(Auld Lang Syne)*

Chapter 15

Songs That Ad Up

The Power of the Pun

A panel of doctors has concluded that punning is good for people. An energetic round of pun and games each day colors the cheeks, puffs up the lungs, firms the muscles, fortifies the immune system, stabilizes blood sugar levels, adds endorphins to the brain and T-cells to the immune system, aerates the capillaries, reduces stress hormones and toxins, dulls pain and inflammation, and tickles the funny bone.

Incorporating puns into your life will give you the energy and endurance to play twice the hours of tennis or golf as you could if your life were punless. So scientists now advise: *Keep on the punny side, always on the punny side. Keep on the punny side of life* and *Double your play, sure; double your puns.*

An Oscar Oscar

The great German actress Brunhilda Von Divagruber had achieved everything she wanted in life but for one honor: She'd never won an Academy Award.

One day she was called by the great director Meyer Schmidtenlager and asked to review a new script he had. She read the script and immediately rejected it. "Iss nicht my type of script, Meyer, and I'll not do it."

"But honeykins," he cried, "it's a wonderful script."

"I didn't say it vasn't vunderful or goot, but I'll not do it."

"But sweetiekins," Meyer continued, "with my direction and your acting and name, the film will make us millions."

"More geldt I don't need. Ich do nicht like the script."

"But, darling, don't you see? With my connections, I can almost guarantee you an Academy Award for your performance."

Brunhilda thought a moment then agreed, musing, "Oh, *I'd luff to be an Oscar winner, Meyer!*"

Witchful Thinking

A young man fell in love with a very lovely young lady. Unfortunately she did not return the feeling. In desperation he went and visited a group of witches to ask for a love potion. He approached the local witch group and asked for a love potion to slip to the reluctant lass.

They informed him that they no longer provided such an item. It was highly unethical to administer a potion to someone without her permission. They did have an alternate solution. They sold him a bottle of small white pellets. He was to bury one in her yard every night at midnight for a month, until they were all gone.

He returned to the witches six weeks later, excited and thankful. He and the young lady were to wed in a month. He was ecstatic and wanted to know how the spell had worked.

The witches explained, *"Nothin' says lovin' like something from the coven, and pills buried says it best!"*

Breakfast in Bed

A married couple awoke early one Sunday morning to find their young daughter standing at their bedside. As was customary, she eagerly brought the morning paper to her parents' room. However, this particular morning, she had brought more than just the morning paper.

Proudly, she handed both her mother and her father their personal coffee mugs, grinning with pride at her resourcefulness and thoughtfulness. As they each thankfully took their mugs, they found not coffee, but six little green plastic army men, carefully arranged in each.

Curious, her Mother asked the obvious. Beaming with pride at having gone to such lengths to brighten her parents' morning, the little cherub replied, "Mommy, everybody knows that *the best part of waking up is soldiers in your cup."*

Pier Pressure

John and Mary were walking along the shore one Sunday afternoon when they spotted a dock projecting into the harbor. They decided to walk to the end of the dock and sit down to rest.

Mary, in her infinite boredom, suggested to John, "While we walk to the end of the dock, why don't you count the number of slats used to build it, and I'll count the number of slits between the slats?"

John replied, "Okay, I will count the slats, and you will count the slits."

So the couple merrily trooped down the dock. John counted, "One slat!"

Mary counted, "One slit!"

"Two slats!"

"Two slits!"

And, well, you know how the natural numbers work. Eventually John and Mary approached the end of the dock.

"327 slats!"

"327 slits!"

"328 slats!"

They had reached the end of the dock. Mary was puzzled.

"John, there are no more slits. What does it mean?"

John turned to Mary and said, *"When you're out of slits, you're out of pier."*

Working for Scale

Timmy and Johnny were having a discussion on who had the greater quantity of tasks to perform around the house. Among those mentioned were dish-drying, lawn-mowing, garden-weeding, pet-feeding, litter-box duty, and garbage removal. The list seemed endless.

This argument was going nowhere fast. They

brought it to Timmy's fourteen-year-old sister for adjudication. She thought for a few minutes and then suggested that they make a balance scale; for each task each could name for which he was responsible, he could place a brick on his side of the scale.

At this moment Johnny's mother looked over the fence at the contraption. When Annie explained what she had had the boys do, Mother nodded knowingly. *"Have a chore weigh!"*

A Moving Experience

Hymie Goldstein owned a fleet of moving vans. He was devoted to his moving business, not only handling customers and keeping the books, but schlepping furniture and other belongings from one location to another. Business boomed.

In dire need of more personnel, Hymie conducted public sessions that described his business and attempted to attract new employees. In one session, Hymie was speaking to three potential recruits – a fitness freak who loved to climb mechanical stairs, a fellow with a wasting disease, and a young woman really into hip hop. Hoping to hire all three, Hymie explained, *"I'm a schlepper, you're a stepper, he's a leper, she is hepper. Wouldn't you like to be a schlepper, too?"*

What a Racket

For six years running, Hugh Acton was the county tennis champ. But this year he ran into the monster, a six-foot-six inch kid who'd recently played college tennis. The young fellow was a terrific player and had run his lead out to 5-3 in the third set when the match was called for the day due to rain.

As they came off the court the press was all over the defending and floundering champ. "What's your problem with this kid? How come you can't take him out?"

The answer was that Hugh couldn't break his opponent's serve, which seemed to crash down from the heavens like a meteor. The kid had seven aces on the afternoon, and Acton had never come close to breaking serve, while losing his twice. "I swear, tomorrow is gonna be different. I'll just have to come out and beat the kid's serve. If I can't do it, I won't win."

The morning papers blared the headline *HUGH TO SERVICE BREAK TODAY.*

Pulling Our Eyes over the Wool

Pierre Rostand, a famous cuisinaire, published a magazine and wrote a column in it detailing various cooking methods. One of his most popular columns mentioned a form of cooking referred to in the Bible, with specific application to a female sheep.

The magazine's marketing branch came up with a great idea. They offered each of their readers a free copy of Chef Pierre's article. To be on the safe side, the recipe and instructions were accompanied by an antacid tablet chosen by Pierre himself. The advertisements for the package announced, *"See the ewe essay and your chef's Rolaid."*

This'll Krill You

Krill are tiny planktonlike crustaceans that are a primary source of food for baleen whales. A family of Daddy Whale, Mommy Whale, and their whale children loved to feast on these crustaceans. In preparing a typical meal, Mommy Whale found that mashing these crustaceans into a thick paste made the perfect repast, supplemented by a healthy portion of crab-shell. Cheerfully, Mother Whale would cluck to her family, *"Krill cream, a brittle crab will do you!"*

A Sonnet

The king must send a messenger to tell
his love that he would marry her. Between
the kingdoms there's a valley. All know well
the Jolly Yellow Giant can be seen
plucking away the riders who would cross.
The Duke tries to deliver, a yellow hand
crushes him 'tween index, thumb. The loss
does not deter the king. An Earl goes and
suffers the same, as does a valiant knight.
A page then volunteers to try. That day
he goes on foot, moves swiftly, never lingers.
The giant's hand just misses. The king's plight
has taught him this — always *let your pages do the walking through the yellow fingers!*

The Answers, My Friend

The Power of the Pun: "Keep on the sunny side" (*Keep on the Sunny Side* by A. P, Carter and Gary Garrett; "Double your pleasure" (*Double Your Pleasure* by Myron Edward and Mike Chon, Doublemint Gum)

An Oscar Oscar: "I'd love to be an Oscar Meyer wiener"(*The Weiner Song* by Richard D. Trentlage, Oscar Meyer Meats)

Witchful Thinking: "Nothing says lovin' like something from the oven, and Pillsbury says it best" (*Pillsbury Says It Best,* Pillsbury Baking Products)

Breakfast in Bed: "The best part of waking up is Folger's in your cup" (Folger's Coffee)

Pier Pressure: "When you're out of Schlitz, you're out of beer" (Schlitz Beer)

Working for Scale: "Have it your way" (*Have It Your Way,* Burger King Restaurants)

A Moving Experience: "I'm a Pepper, you're a Pepper, he's a Pepper, she's a Pepper. Wouldn't you like to be a Pepper, too?" (Dr. Pepper soft drink)

What a Racket: "You deserve a break today" (*You Deserve a Break* by Kevin Gavin and Sid Woolshin, McDonald's Restaurants)

Pulling Our Eyes over the Wool: "See the USA in your Chevrolet" (*See the USA* by Leon Carr and Leo Corday, Chevrolet automobile)

This'll Krill You: "Brylcreem, a little dab will do ya" (*Brylcreem, a Little Dab Will Ya* by John P. Atherton and Hanley Norins, Brylcreem Hair Cream)

A Sonnet: "Let your fingers do the walking through the Yellow Pages." (*Let Your Fingers Do the Walking,* A. T. & T.)

Chapter 16

Super Agile Punch Lines

Some song lines strike the ear and the imagination in a special way and generate not just a single punch line, but many. In this chapter and the two that follow we, your puckish – but never puke-ish — pun pals, present the three most spectacular sagas of multiple punch lines we have ever encountered.

We'll start with *supercalifragilisticexpialidocious,* a thirty-four-letter word invented for the film *Mary Poppins* (1964) and immortalized in the song by Richard M. Sherman and Robert B. Sherman. Now sharpen your pun cells and have fun with these serial thrillers.

The Gandhi Man Can

One of the greatest men of the twentieth century was Mahatma Gandhi. His denial of the earthly pleasures included the fact that he never wore anything on his feet. He walked barefoot everywhere. Moreover, he ate so little that he developed delicate health and very bad breath. Therefore, he became known as a *super callused fragile mystic hexed by halitosis.*

Mary Pops In

Mary Poppins, the magical British nanny, was travelling home, but due to worsening weather, she decided to stop at a hotel for the night. She approached the receptionist and asked for a room.

"Certainly, madam," he replied courteously.

"Is the restaurant open still?" inquired Mary.

"Sorry, no," came the reply, "but room service is available all night. Would you care to select something from this menu?"

Mary smiled and took the menu and perused it. "Hmm, I would like cauliflower cheese please. And may I have breakfast in bed?" asked Mary politely.

The receptionist nodded and smiled.

"In that case, I would love a couple of poached eggs, please," Mary mused.

After confirming the order, Mary signed in and went up to her room. The night passed uneventfully and next morning Mary came down early to check out. The same guy was still on the desk. "Morning, madam. Sleep well?"

"Yes, thank you," Mary replied.

"Food to your liking?"

"Well, I have to say the cauliflower cheese was exceptional, I don't think I have had better. Shame about the eggs though. They really weren't that nice at all," replied Mary truthfully.

"Oh, well, perhaps you could contribute these thoughts to our Guest Comments Book. We are always looking to improve our service and would value your opinion," said the receptionist.

"Okay, I will, thanks!" replied Mary, who then checked out, paused awhile, then scribbled a comment into the book. Waving, she left to continue her journey. Curious, the receptionist picked up the book to see the comment Mary had written: *"Super cauliflower cheese, but eggs were quite atrocious!"*

The Breathalyzer

Many people don't realize that Mary Poppins, who went around using her own special magic to solve families' problems, finally retired from the nanny business. Wondering what to do, she decided to use her considerable skills for magical incantation to live a life of comfort in the warm California sun. Thus, she moved to California and entered the business of fortune telling.

However, Mary Poppins was not a traditional fortune teller. She eschewed the usual, time-worn methods of soothsaying. She spoke no magic charms over frog entrails or rabbit innards. She never needed to keep a stock of eye-of-newt potions. She ignored the powers of the Ouija board. She never consulted the stars and constellations. Astrology was not her forte, so she cast no horoscopes. Neither did she read palms or bother herself with lifelines and heartlines. She would have nothing to do with Tarot cards either.

But Mary Poppins did hit upon a sure-fire, successful method of divining the future and revealing all that is arcane and secret. She would take a whiff of breath and by analyzing her client's exhalations, she could tell his or her fortune, and she could do this flawlessly. People flocked to consult Mary Poppins out on the West Coast, and she was an outstanding success as the *Super California Mystic. Expert Halitosis*.

Mono a Mono

Charlie went to an infectious disease specialist, whom his internist had recommended. The specialist started taking Charlie's history. His symptoms included swollen neck glands, difficulty swallowing, a sore throat, a low grade fever, and fatigue. The doctor advised him that he had mononucleosis. "I've developed another symptom," Charlie told the ID specialist. "Besides the ones that I described a few days ago, I'm also farting constantly. Do you think that it could be related to my condition?"

The doctor informed him that passing gas was an unusual indication to be associated with the disease and medical science had no name for the particular affliction.

Exasperated, Charlie replied, "That's *super, call it flatulistic mononucleosis.*"

Lip Service

A young woman, extraordinarily attractive in personality, character, and presentation, was suffering from an illness that made her lips cracked and sore. The slightest movement of her mouth caused pain and embarrassment. Her condition, though not cured, was somewhat relieved by the application of a medication prescribed by her physician.

The instructions on the prescription were to apply the medication once a day, but the young woman found that more frequent applications were palatable and effective.

After exhausting her supply, she returned to the doctor's office for another one. The receptionist announced the arrival of the returning patient to the doctor: "It's the *super gal with fragile lips expecting extra doses.*"

I Have a Little List

A man went to the grocery store to buy canned soup, a cauliflower, a rubber band to keep his refrigerator door from staying open, a dozen eggs, a legume, and something for the garlic on his breath.

His grocery list read: *"Soup, a cauli . . . , fridge elastic, eggs, pea, halitosis."*

Soccer It to Us

Followers of the tiny Scottish soccer club Inverness Caledonian-Thistle refer to the club as "Caley." The team delighted fans last winter when it eliminated heavily favored Glasgow Celtic 3-1 in the Scottish Cup. The upset prompted this headline in the British tabloid the *Sun: SUPER CALEY GO BALLISTIC; CELTICS ARE ATROCIOUS.*

The Bull Whisperer

My girlfriend could talk to the animals — and they could talk to her as well (thank you very much, Dr. Doolittle).

She used her teacher-child-psych skills in college to carry this capability one step further: By talking to beasts in a soothing fashion, she could actually hypnotize them and offer post-hypnotic behavior modification.

She discovered this quite accidentally one afternoon as a teenager when her family dog, persisting in defending the entire neighborhood, was nearly hit by a car. She taught him the limits of the property and explained that the limits of the property were not only all that he had to defend, but, additionally, that he shouldn't stray beyond the boundaries.

Word got out about her skills, and all kinds of people with all types of pets came to her for behavior modification.

One day, a local dairy farmer asked her to tame his prize-winning bull. This was a special bovine because its offspring were superior milk producers. At the same time, getting this bull to calm down enough for even three farmhands to lead him into the mating pasture made the farmer frequently wonder if it was worth the trouble. So he asked my girlfriend if she could administer some post-hypnotic suggestion about tranquility and the rewards of that pasture.

My girlfriend gently approached the bull, talking quietly to him all the time. But he snorted and ran and shook his head and generally refused to hear anything she was saying. After several hours of this, she had to admit defeat, went to the farmer, gave him his money back, and explained that apparently this particular animal had such trepidation, nay, downright fear, of listening to her, that it wasn't going to work.

All would have been well, except that my girlfriend was so traumatized by the loss of her power (such failure had never happened before) that it actually damaged her ability. She could no longer concentrate on the animal at hand, couldn't begin to hypnotize it, and couldn't understand what they were saying any more. So she had to give it up. 'Twas the *super cattle, 'fraid to listen, hexed my gal's hypnosis.*

Chapter 17

The Chatty Choo Choo

Back in 1941, Harry Warren and Mack Gordon cre-ated the hit song *Chattanooga Choo Choo* for the movie *Sunrise Serenade*. Today, the choo choo keeps chugging along and stopping again and again at Pun-sylvania Station. Please don't feel railroaded as we present the most fun-omenal set of verbivo-rous variations ever loosed upon the world.

He Went Cataway!

The famous singing cowboy Roy Rogers went bathing in a creek. He took off his clothes, including his brand new boots. Along came a cougar, and, attracted to the smell of new leather, the critter began chomping on one of Roy's boots. Roy's wife, Dale Evans, entered the scene, pulled out her trusty six-shooter, and fired it in the air, chasing the cougar away. Dale turned to her husband and asked, *"Pardon me, Roy. Is that the cat that chewed your new shoe?"*

What's Gnu?

As he was leaving the zoo, a visitor walked by the gnu cage and noticed an unkempt gnu sitting morosely in a corner. Outside the cage was a large bamboo shoot with teeth marks on it. Thinking the gnu might have thrown it out of the cage, the visitor turned to an attendant and asked, *"Pardon me, boy, is that the shoddy gnu's bamboo shoot?"*

There Will Never Be Another Pew

A Jewish gentleman had a son who became a talkative New Age guru. After a while, his congregation, out of appreciation, bought a fancy new bench for their church, and he sat in it often, along with other worshippers.

One day the father decided that he wanted to visit his son, so he walked into the church, but the guru happened to be absent. Deciding to wait on the bench for his son's return, he walked over to the fanciest bench in the church and said to the person sitting there: *"Pardon me, goy, is that the chatty guru's new pew?"*

Talking Point

Not to be outdone by the "Snap, crackle, pop!" of the cereal industry, a confectionary chemist invented a candy that talks when you bite into it. So if you hear the words "yummy, yummy slurp, slurp, I'm so good" coming from the mouth of a chomping youngster, you can ask, *"Pardon me, boy, is that the chatty nougat you chew?"*

A Ford in the Future

According to a wholly unsubstantiated rumor repeated in White House circles shortly after former President Nixon retired to his San Clemente estate in disgrace, Mr. Nixon telephoned Gerald Ford, his successor. When the new president got on the line, Mr. Nixon is unreliably reported to have said, *"Pardon me, boy. This is the chap who knew to choose you."*

I'm So Afreud

A new patient, one Mrs. L, was ushered into the office of Sigmund Freud in 19th-century Vienna. At first Mrs. L. was ill at ease in the presence of the great man and extremely hesitant about explaining her troubles. Dr. Freud suggested that she lie down on the couch and say anything, whatever came into her head.

Mrs. L., relaxing despite herself, started to talk, at first haltingly. Then, speaking compulsively, she found herself revealing her single greatest fear — that she was going crazy. Suddenly, feeling terribly self-conscious, Mrs. L, stopped in midsentence, looked over at the great doctor, and asked, *"Pardon me, Freud, but is my chatter really cuckoo?"*

TV or Not TV

An aspiring videographer bought one of those new high-end digital cameras, and it really did improve the quality of his work. The equipment boosted his sales and generally made him very happy in his career, so much so that he could not stop bragging in song. His new business theme ditty started, *"Pardon my joy. This is the cam that did my new shoot!"*

Material Girl

On the set of a new *Thin Man* movie, a prop man noticed Myrna Loy carrying a swatch of material in her hand. Said he: *"Pardon me, Loy, is that the shantung that's the new clue?"*

Light My Fire

Officer O'Malley was sent to investigate a fire. He emerged from the burnt-out building with a fedora in one hand and a revolver in the other hand and was heard to say to his young assistant: *"Arson, me boy. This hat and gat will do for new clues."*

Making a Mark

In one episode of *The Real McCoys,* Walter Brennan went into town to Louie's tattoo parlor to get himself tattooed. Little Luke, seeing the resulting design, asked, *"Grandpa McCoy, is that the tattoo you had Lou do?"*

The Two Georges

In 2020, when Boy George had become too old for the rock music circuit, he decided to take advantage of his notoriety to enter politics and was duly elected as governor of Tennessee.

As part of the duties of his new office, he was touring the state's prison facilities, when lo, there behind bars was George Lucas! Lucas had fallen from his fame and wealth, become a drunk, and ended up unknown, in jail, after killing a man in a bar-room brawl.

Governor George immediately offered to commute the filmmaker's sentence, but insisted that one of his dreams was to have been in one of the *Star Wars* films. Fulfilling this dream was the *quid pro quo* that would need to be paid. Lucas reluctantly agreed, but only with the additional stipulation: as he could now only work when well lubricated, he must be supplied with the finest whiskey Tennessee had to offer.

The first day on the set, prison guards escorted Lucas to the Governor, who held out a glass of clear amber fluid. The director asked the governor, *"Pardon me Boy, is that the shot I need to shoot you?"*

The Wine Ain't Fine

A wine distributor, who had the exclusive franchise on an exclusive French vintage, was informed that an American counterfeit was on the market. So he set out to learn where it was being made. He looked long and hard and was getting discouraged, when, footsore and weary, he peeked into a warehouse and saw bottles of the fake stuff. Happy because his long search was over, he turned to the warehouseman and asked, *"Pardon my joy. Is that the chateau neuf you brew, too?"*

On the Mend

An hour before a prima ballerina was to go on stage to perform her role as the Sugar Plum Fairy in *The Nutcracker Suite*, her dress began to come apart. Fortunately, she recalled a rare formula for making a fixative that would repair the damage and save the day.

She quickly stirred copper and tin together to make brass, allowed the mixture to set, and then added some gooey baby food to the concoction. She applied the results to the torn part of her, and incredibly the dress held together until she completed the performance.

Encouraged by the success of her strategy, she shared the instructions with her fellow dancers: *Harden alloy, and add the pap to glue your tutu.*

Frosty the No Man

A landlord was put on trial for negligent homicide. It was charged that he failed to provide adequate heat for an apartment, causing the tenant to freeze to death. The landlord replied that the loss of heat was due to defects in the design of the apartment, which he could neither foresee nor control. And, in any case, the deceased brought his demise on himself by walking around naked in the middle of the winter.

The landlord was convicted, but his mother appealed to the governor, saying, "*Pardon my boy. It was the flat that slew the nude dude.*"

The Cat/Bird Heat

My son Tom had developed a friendly relationship with a poet who lived next door. The poet was something of an eccentric who lived by himself, with an Angora cat and a bird that looked like it belonged in a house in the Black Forest.

One day my son and the poet went out together for a walk in the park. When they returned they discovered that, whatever had occurred, the cat was wild-eyed and appeared ready to attack, and the bird had escaped its cage and was flying around the room screaming its call at the top of its lungs.

While the poet made snake-like sounds at his four-legged pet, Tom popped open the door on the microwave oven. The bird flew in; he shut the door; and, unfortunately from habit, he then pressed the "Start" button — and cooked the bird.

This whole incident can be described by: *"Bard and my boy hissed at the cat and nuked a cuckoo."*

Chapter 18

What's Amore?

For many years now, there has been circulating a continuously expanding poem. Its leaping-off place is the first verse of *That's Amore*, the song by Harry Warren and Jack Brooks made famous by crooner Dean Martin:

When the moon hits your eye
Like a big pizza pie,
That's amore.

Around the turn of the century we are living in, Frank Rubin, of Wappinger Falls, New York, came up with the idea of writing some additional verses and inviting others to contribute theirs to his Web site. Soon, the science-fiction writer Spider Robinson picked up the idea on his site. Sure enough, something about the rhythm of the lines and the sounds of that last line inspired punsters to soar hilariously from the launch pad of the original. Sing along with the best of the take-offs:

When an eel bites your heel
And a twinge you do feel,
That's a moray.

If a sea creature did
Make you scream, "Oh, you squid!":
Calamary.

When our habits are strange
And our customs deranged,
That's our mores.

When the heather and grass
Together they mass,
That's a moor, eh?

When Othello's poor wife
Gets carved up with a knife,
That's a Moor, eh?

When a Japanese knight
Draws a sword for a fight,
That's Samurai.

He tells jokes; he's a ham.
His last name's Amsterdam;
That's a Morey.

When two patterns combine
In a way serpentine,
That's a moire.

If through *King Kong* you've sat,
Rent the flick *Vampire Bat,*
And see more Wray.

Ray Charles gained so much fame
That his fans screamed his name:
"Sing some more, Ray!"

When the yup bought his Deere,
All the neighbors did hear,
"That's a mower, eh!"

If you want to have fun
By being top gun,
Join NRA.

 A New Zealander man
With a permanent tan:
That's a Maori

If your vitamins be
Mainly C, D, and E,
Take some more A

When Canadians show
You their mothers, they go,
"That's my mawr, eh."

He stole bases for thrills,
And his last name is Wills.
That's a Maury.

When you build up a bond
Playing one wicked blonde,
That's De Mornay!

When a camera just might
Catch your halo of light,
That's an aura.

When you might make a feast
For some alien beast,
That's Sigourney.

When Canucks start to fight
With their guns in the night,
That's a war, eh?

When you're eating with cows
And the cuisine just wows,
That's some more hay.

Once your girlfriend was hot.
Now she's wife, and she's not
Anymore, eh?

The Harry Potter saga
Makes readers go gaga.
That's a story!

Watching Zorro run through
All the bad guys helps you
Learn some swordplay.

The Ants Are My Friends

Avocado mashed up
And dished out from a cup:
Guacamole

He's from over the pond —
Played both Templar and Bond.
That's R. Moore, eh?

An old Aussie bird
In prehistory occurred.
That's a Moa, eh?

When Ms. Stewart tops weeds
With gold sesame seeds,
That's potpourri.

When the top-ranking Whig
Calls the P.M. a prig,
That's a Tory.

Bush, G.W., won
A hard-fought election
From one Gore, A.

When rangers in hoods
Lead treks through the woods,
That's a foray.

When an area stocks
A great number of rocks,
That's a quarry.

What's Amore?

When you get in a fight
With a guy of great height,
You'll be sore, eh?

When a sting ray is all
That they sell at a mall,
That's a mall ray.

When doc scans your head
On a magnetic bed,
That's M-R-I.

Our serial pun
Its course it has run.
So no more play.

Chapter 19

Waggy Shaggy Dog Tails

The set-up puns you have been reading are sometimes erroneously called Shaggy Dog Stories.
That label is incorrect because "Shaggy Dog" should
be reserved for a specific type of joke.

Do you remember your first overnight camping
experience? In the evening you might have sat
around a campfire near the camp pool, where your
counselor spent twenty minutes or more telling a
story that had a punch line so inane or trivial that the
campers picked up the counselor and threw him fully

dressed into the pool.

Or you may have been at a slumber party where one of the girls spent ages in telling a story that had an ending that was such a letdown that the rest of the girls threw their pillows at her.

These events describe true Shaggy Dog Stories. Two characteristics must be present to enshrine a set-up pun in the pantheon of Shaggy Dog Stories. First, the narrative must be excruciatingly prolonged by the repetition of events and gratuitous side trips to make the story become tedious before it reaches the anticipated denouement. Second, the *pun*ch line must evoke such a letdown, that instead of laughing, you would like to attack the teller for wasting so much of your time.

The original Shaggy Dog Story tells – interminably – of a northern Canadian trapper named Sam and his mongrel dog Rover. One day Sam read that an ailing and eccentric millionaire was offering half his fortune to the person who brought him the shaggiest dog. The narrator of the tale inserts as many horrific episodes as possible about icy crevasses, blizzards, starvation, polar bears, thin ice, thick snow — anything to make the journey as difficult and as courageous as possible and extends the story unnecessarily.

Here's the original ending:

As Sam drew nearer to civilization, he learned with great relief that the search for a dog continued and that the millionaire's mansion lay at the top of a steep hill just visible on the horizon.

Up Sam and Rover climbed, tired and tattered, arriving eventually at the huge oak-studded front door.

The Ants Are My Friends

Raising a weather-beaten hand, Sam tugged at the wrought iron bell-pull. Distantly the bell clanged. The door opened and a butler stood in the doorway.

"I've come about the shaggy dog story in this newspaper," said Sam, carefully drawing out the clipping from his innermost pocket and offering Rover's leash to the manservant.

Silently the butler withdrew with the dog. Sam listened to his footsteps cross the vast hall and ascended the massive circular staircase. He waited patiently on the doorstep, dreaming of the luxury soon to be his. At last the butler reappeared. Solemnly he handed back the dog.

"Not that shaggy," he said, and shut the door.

Some purists assert that a true Shaggy Dog Story cannot end in a pun. In this chapter we lay before you two examples that prove this view is bogus.

Caveat lector: You are forewarned. Most people hate true Shaggy Dog Stories. If you fall into that group, you may wish to skip this chapter. But if we have aroused your curiosity, start reading the two Shaggy Dogs that follow to see that musical set-up puns can be as shaggy as any other breed of narrative.

A Hokey Story

A guy spent five years traveling all around the world making a documentary on native dances. Finally, he had on film every single native dance of every indigenous culture in the world.

He wound up in Alice Springs and popped into a pub for a well-earned beer. He got talking to one of the local Aborigines and told him about his project.

The Aborigine asked the guy what he thought of the "Butcher's Dance."

The guy was a bit confused and asked, "Butcher's Dance? What's that?" "What? You no see Butcher's Dance?"

"No, I've never heard of it."

"Oh mate. You crazy. How you say you film every native dance if you no see Butcher's Dance?"

"Um, I got a corroboree on film just the other

week. Is that what you mean?"

"No, no, not corroborree. Butcher's Dance much more important than corroborree."

"Oh, well how can I see this Butcher's Dance then?"

"Mate, Butcher's Dance right in bush. Many days travel to go see Butcher's Dance."

"Look, I've been everywhere from the forests of the Amazon, to deepest darkest Africa, to the frozen wastes of the Arctic filming these dances. Nothing will prevent me from recording this one last dance."

"Okay, mate. You drive north along highway towards Darwin. After you drive 197 miles, you see dirt track veer off to left. Follow dirt track for 126 miles 'til you see big huge dead gum tree – biggest tree you ever see. Here you gotta leave car, cuz much too rough for driving."

"You strike out due west into setting sun. You walk three days 'til you hit creek. You follow this creek to Northwest. After two days you find where creek flows out of rocky mountains. Much too difficult to cross mountains here though."

"You now head south for half day till you see pass through mountains. Pass very difficult, very dangerous. Take two, maybe three days to get through rocky pass."

"When through, head north-west for four days till reach big huge rock, twenty-foot high and shaped like man's head. From rock, walk due west for two days and you find village. Here you see Butcher's Dance."

So the guy grabbed his camera crew and equipment and headed out. After a couple of hours he found the dirt track. The track was in a shocking state, and he was forced to crawl along at a snails pace, so he didn't reach the tree until dusk and had to set up camp for the night.

He set out bright and early the following morning. His spirits were high, and he was excited about the prospect of capturing on film this mysterious dance that he had never heard mention of before. True to the directions he has been given, he reached the creek after three days and followed it for another two until they reached the rocky mountains.

The merciless sun was starting to take its toll by this time, and our hero's spirits were starting to flag. Wearily he trudged on until he found the pass through the hills. Nothing was going prevent him from completing his life's dream.

The mountains proved to be every bit as treacherous as their guide said, and at times they almost despaired of getting their bulky equipment through. But after three and a half days of backbreaking effort, they finally forced their way clear and continued their long trek.

When they reached the huge rock, four days later, their water was running low, and their feet were covered with blisters. They steeled themselves and headed out on the last leg of their journey.

Two days later they staggered into the village, where the natives fed them and gave them fresh water. He began to feel like a new man.

Once he recovered enough, our hero went before the village chief and told him that he had come to film their Butcher's Dance.

"Oh mate. Very bad you come today. Butcher's Dance last night. You too late. You miss dance."

"Well, when do you hold the next dance?"

172 The Ants Are My Friends

"Not till next year."

"Well, I've come all this way. Couldn't you just hold an extra dance for me, tonight?"

"No, no, no! Butcher's Dance very holy. Only hold once a year. If hold more, gods get very angry and destroy village! You want see Butcher's Dance, you come back next year."

The guy was devastated. But he had no other option but to head back to civilization and back home.

The following year, he flew back to Australia and, determined not to miss out again, set out a week earlier than last time. He was quite willing to spend a week in the village before the dance was to be performed in order to ensure he witnessed it.

However, right from the start things went wrong. Heavy rains that year turned the dirt track to mud, and the car got bogged every few miles, finally forcing him to abandon the vehicle and slog through the mud on foot almost half the distance to the tree.

Our hero reached the creek and the mountains without any further hitch, but halfway through the ascent of the mountain he was struck by a fierce storm, which raged for several days, during which he was forced to cling forlornly to the mountainside until the storm subsided.

Then, before our hero traveled a mile out from the mountains, the intrepid explorer sprained his ankle badly, which slowed down the rest of the journey to the rock and then the village. Eventually, having lost all sense of how long he had been traveling, he staggered into the village at about noon.

"The Butcher's Dance!" gasped the guy. "Please don't tell me I'm too late!" The chief recognized him and said, "No, white fella. Butcher's Dance performed tonight. You come just in time."

Relieved beyond measure, our hero spent the rest of the afternoon setting up his equipment, preparing to capture the night's ritual on celluloid. As dusk fell, the natives started to cover their bodies in white paint and adorn themselves in all manner of bird's feathers and animal skins.

Once darkness settled fully over the land, the natives formed a circle around a huge roaring fire. A deathly hush descended on the performers and spectators alike as a wizened old figure with elaborate swirling designs covering his entire body entered the circle and began to chant. Some sort of witch doctor or medicine man, figured our hero, and he whispered to the chief. "What's he doing?"

"Hush," whispered the chief. "You first white man ever to see most sacred of our rituals. Must remain silent. Holy man asks that the spirits of the dream world watch as we demonstrate our devotion to them through our dance and, if they like our dancing, will they be so gracious as to watch over us and protect us for another year."

The chanting of the holy man reached a stunning crescendo before he removed himself from the circle. From somewhere the rhythmic pounding of drums boomed out across the land and the natives began to sway to the stirring rhythm.

The guy became caught up in the fervor of the moment himself. He now realized beyond all doubt that his wait had not been in vain. He was about to witness the ultimate performance of rhythm and movement ever conceived by mankind.

The chief strode to his position in the circle and, in a big booming voice, sang, *"You butch yer right*

arm in. You butch yer right arm out. You butch yer
right arm in and you shake it all about!"

Here's our second and, thankfully (you must
surely be thinking), last Shaggy Dog Story with a
musically lyrical crescendo. To gain additional insight
into what makes a shaggy dog story shaggy, com-
pare this version with the first tale in "Code of Eth-
nics."

Big Bird

This chap and his wife loved Budgerigars, and
they went to a pet shop and bought one. They
bought a cage and some seed and took it home.
They filled the seed bowl, and the baby budgie
hopped onto the rim and in one suck swallowed the
lot. It then swelled to twice its size.

They refilled the bowl, and it swallowed that in
one enormous suck. It again swelled to twice its size.
Every time they filled the bowl the bird just hopped
onto the rim and with one suck emptied it and then
immediately grew to twice its size.

Well, the couple thought that this was a laugh,
until the second day when they placed a large bowl
in the cage and filled it with a whole box of seed, and
the Budgie just sucked the lot up in one enormous
swallow and then grew to twice its size and showed
that it could also talk. It bellowed in a stentorian
voice, "More seed! More seed! More seed!" making
all the windows shake and the crockery rattle.

The bird kept it up till the bowl was filled and just
as fast emptied. Each time the bird then shouted for
"More seed! More seed! More seed!" After a day
and a night, the couple realized that it was an all-day

and all-night job — and very expensive, because the bird was gobbling seed faster than they were earning the money to buy it.

They went back to the pet shop and told the shopkeeper what had happened. He immediately said, "No, no, you can't return the bird!"

The man said, "We don't want to return it because we love the thing, but what can we do? It's now so big that it's out of its cage and fills the sitting room and just keeps demanding 'More seed! More seed! More seed!'"

The shopkeeper answered, "This is an abnormal bird known in budgie circles as a Rarey Bird because they are mutants and they just eat and eat and get bigger and bigger and live for years and years. You've got a problem because you cannot kill them. Bullets just go into them, and they digest the lead and just get bigger. Poison the same. They are too big to strangle or to stab or beat to death, and so you just have to live with it!"

The man said, "But we just cannot go on like this. We're just exhausted feeding it and working to earn its food!"

The shopkeeper said, "Yeah, I know. That's why we never ever take Rarey Birds back. They're a real problem. The only way to kill them is to drop them from a great height, like from an airplane, because they are too big to fly. The crash into the ground kills them instantly. The trouble is that by the time you find out what they are, it is too late. They are too heavy to get up in a plane. You will just have to buy all of my seed and put up with it!"

The couple put up with it for another week, and by this time they had grown even fonder than ever of the Budgie. They even called it Rarey and it answered to its name by shouting, "More seed for Rarey! More seed for Rarey!"

The couple sold the car, they sold the washing machine, they sold the fridge, they sold the furniture, they sold the garden shed, and they sold the lawn-mower. They became so poor that eventually they couldn't even afford another packet of seed.

The man said, "We are going to have to kill Rarey! We still have the wheelbarrow and two planks, and we will have to struggle up to the top of the mountain and tip it over the precipice and let it smash down to the ground."

Well, the wife cried and so did the man, but it was inevitable and so they laid the two planks on the wheelbarrow and using long poles as fulcrums, finally got the Rarey bird onto the planks where it immediately started to shout, "More Seed for Rarey! More seed for Rarey! More Seed for Rarey!"

The couple went through sheer hell to transport the Rarey Bird to the top of the mountain. They had to hitch pulleys to trees and pull the Rarey up to each tree and then start all over again. And all of the time there was this stentorian bellowing from the bird: "More seed for Rarey! More seed for Rarey! More seed for Rarey!"

Well, affection for pets has to stop somewhere. By the time they finally struggled to the top of the mountain they were actually looking forward to shutting the poor thing's beak forever.

They just had one final hurdle to overcome. How could they tip the wheelbarrow, two planks and the Rarey Bird high enough so that the bird went over the precipice? They solved this by using the same ploy that the ancient Britains used to build Stone-henge. They jacked up the rear of the wheelbarrow and placed stones and earth under the legs. They repeated this until the wheelbarrow, planks, and the Rarey Bird were tilted at an angle so acute that the slightest push would tip it all over the precipice.

The couple walked around the wheelbarrow to the edge of the precipice and stood looking down. The man said, "Wow, some drop! That must be at least 2,000 feet from the edge to the ground below!"

They stood there in silence for a moment and then became aware that the Rarey Bird was no longer shouting, "More seed for Rarey!" but was singing. They had never heard it sing before and stood quietly listening.

Their big pet was now singing, *"Oh, it's a long way to tip a Rarey. It's a long way to go!"*

The Answers, My Friends

A Hokey Story: "You put your right arm in, you put your right arm out, you put your right arm in, and you shake it all about" (*Hokey Pokey* by Roland LaPrise, Chuck Macak, and Tafft Baker)

Big Bird: "It's a long way to Tipperary. It's a long way to go" (*It's a Long Way to Tipperary* by Jack Judge and Harry Williams)

Chapter 20

Test: A Round of Set-Ups

Someone once wrote that a pun is the lowest form of wit. The authors of this book offer a rebuttal: A pun is the doughiest form of wheat.

Now it's time to wash down all those buns with a round of set-ups. Fill in each blank by supplying the musical *pun*ch line to each story.

1. *Isn't It Romantic?*

The great Romantic poet Percy Shelley was despondent. After banging out poems, odes, and dramas with ease, he had suddenly run up against that which all poets fear more than editorial rejection — writer's block. No matter how hard he tried, nothing came. Page after page of gibberish went into the basket.

Pacing the streets of Oxford one morning, he encountered his friend and fellow poet John Keats. Keats was in fine spirits but soon became solicitous when he heard of Shelley's plight.

"The very thing happened to me last year," said Keats. "Upon the advice of a friend, I visited a small religious retreat, Mount St. Michaela, off the coast of Cornwall. It is run by an order of nuns, and there is nothing to do but listen to the surf and the gulls. In no time at all I was afire to put pen to paper."

"Then I shall do it," vowed Shelley, and he hurried off to make arrangements.

Three days later, after a long, dusty, and tiring coach ride, he arrived in the small coastal village across from the nunnery, and there he hired a skiff to take him over to the island three miles distant. A wind was coming up and the sun was setting as the fisherman methodically pulled the oars, drawing the boat ever nearer. The waves grew angrier, but finally the boat scraped alongside a rock and Shelley jumped ashore. Scrambling up the stone steps, he made his way to the front door of the convent and pounded on the heavy wood. Soon a small window opened and a young woman peered out. "I'm Percy Shelley, and I've come to stay here awhile. Please let me in."

"I'm only a novitiate," a small voice answered. "Mother Superior has retired for the night, and only if I have her signature can I allow you admittance."

"But a storm is coming up, and the boat has gone

The Ants Are My Friends

back to the village," pleaded the poet. "Surely you can authorize it yourself."

"I'm very sorry," answered the young sister. "You have to *wait till the _____, Shelley."*

2. *Par for the Course*

Many sports observers feel that Jack Nicklaus was the greatest golfer ever to play the game. One day Jack was surpassing even his stratospheric level of play, driving each ball off the tee with one stroke and then putting it into the hole with just one more stroke.

After four such holes in a row, when he had driven the ball yet again to within easy reach of the fifth hole, the adoring crowd shouted out to Jack, *"_____ another, _____, in!"*

3. *Rings a Bell*

Long ago, in a small country in Europe, one family had for centuries made all the bells for the churches in the village. Finally, only one member of the bell-making family was left, and he was also the mayor of the town. Feeling threatened by competition, the mayor decreed that no wedding bells might be rung in the village unless they were made by him. He enforced this rule strictly and became known as the Wedding-Bell Czar.

One couple decided to marry without using the czar's bells. They had a friend who owned an ancient Chinese gong, and they used it instead. Shortly after the wedding, a fearsome noise was heard coming from the gong-owner's home. The bride and groom rushed to investigate. "Whatever does that noise mean?" they cried.

"It means," said their friend, wringing his hands, *"That Wedding-Bell Czar's breaking up that _____."*

4. *Doggone*

One of the pups in a breeder's litter of collies had a strange appetite. The odd youngster spurned regular dog food. No meaty tidbits could tempt him, and he hated dog biscuits. Just in time to save the little dog's life, the owner found he would eat nothing but cantaloupes. He doted on them.

His brother pups could not understand this, and they teased him unmercifully. He became the butt of their pranks until his tail would droop and he would whimper and shiver in a corner. His mother, trying to comfort him, called to him: *"Come to me, my _____."*

5. *Gull Meets Buoy*

During the really hard times after his breakup with Cher, Sonny Bono got a job wearing a day-glow life jacket and serving as a shallow-water marker to warn boats. One of the strange, but little known characteristics of this phase of his career is that night never fell while he was on the job; it was clearly a day job. And, he always hoped for a reconciliation with Cher, hoping to hear those words, *"Climb upon my knee, _____."*

Now try writing your own set-up narratives and *pun*ch lines. You may use your punny version of any of the dozen lines below, or you can choose your own song on which to build your joke.

The Ants Are My Friends

Shine on harvest moon, for me and my gal.

There is a house in New Orleans that's called the rising sun.

Hey, Mr. tambourine man, play a song for me.

Birds do it. Bees do it. Even educated fleas do it.

Sometimes you feel like a nut. Sometimes you don't.

Yesterday, all my troubles seemed to far away.

Don't stop thinking about tomorrow.

You are the wind beneath my wings.

Two for tea, and tea for two.

A mighty fortress is our God, a bulwark never failing.

I wish I could shimmy like my sister, Kate.

We will, we will rock you.

The Answers, My Friends

1. *Isn't It Romantic?:* "Wait till the nun shines, Shelley" ("Wait till the sun shines, Nellie," *Wait Till the Sun Shines,* Nellie by Harry Von Tilzer and Andrew B. Sterling)

2. *Par for the Course:* "Putt another, Nicklaus, in" ("Put another nickel in," *Music! Music! Music!* By Stephan Weiss and Bernie Baum)

3. *Rings a Bell:* "That wedding bell czar's breaking up that old gong of mine" ("Those wedding bells are breaking up that old gang of mine," *Wedding Bells are Breaking Up That Old Gang of Mine* by Sammy Fain, Irving Kahal, and William Raskin)

4. *Doggone:* "Come to me, my melon collie baby" ("Come to me, my melancholy baby," *My Melancholy Baby* by Ernie Burnett, George A. Norton, and Maybelle E. Watson)

5. *Gull Meets Buoy:* "Climb upon my knee, Sonny buoy" ("Climb upon my knee, sonny boy," *Sonny Boy* by Ray Henderson, Lew Brown, B.G. De Sylva, and Al Jolson)

Call for Submissions

Now that you have tried writing groaners, you can see how much fun they can be. We would be happy to review any that you create and submit to us. You will retain full ownership of your work, but you authorize us to edit them, post them on the Internet, and/or publish them in a future book. If we do use them, you will be given credit as the owner.

Please e-mail your original puns to Stan Kegel at skegel@socal.rr.com or Richard Lederer at richard.lederer@pobox.com

Credits Where Credits Are Due

We have striven valiantly to track down the sources of each pun in this book that isn't our own creation. It's the kind of task that you enter optimistically and leave misty optically: Many puns whiz around cyberspace unattributed. We know that well because we have seen so many of our own tour de farces materialize on the Internet with no attribution or – weep weep, sob sob, honk honk! – attribution to someone else. Other puns have a name attached, but it's not clear if those people created the arty facts or simply submitted them.

To our pun pals who are in our cites below, we thank you for your genius and willingness to share. To those whom we have somehow neglected to credit, we offer our apologies. We trust you'll be pleased that, albeit anonymously, your lyrical puns sing out from the pages of this book.

Face the Music

What a Drag and *Hot Dogs!* Gary Hallock; *Say Cheese,* Ted Brett; *Gator Aid* and *Blimey! Slimy!* Cynthia MacGregor; *A Stock Answer,* Bradley Williams; *Battle of the Bottles,* Alan B. Combs; *Going Nuts* and *A Mine Is a Terrible Thing,* Chris Cole; *A Ghost Graduate Course,* Sir Richard Burton;

Love Is All You Need

The World Is My Oyster, Ted Brett; *The Gain in Spain,* Himie Koshevoy; *A Lot of Gaul,* Les Dawson; *Mon Amy* and *Tall, Dark, and Hairy,* Bob Levi; *Monkee-ing Around,* Bob Dvorak; *The Eyes of Taxes Are upon You,* Kurt Wenner;

Olden Goldies

A Pun of Biblical Proportions, Don Hauptman; *What's the Good Kurd?* Bob Levi; *Pi in the Sky,* Alan B. Combs: *Against the Grain* Kurt Wenner; *Getting Oriented* Gary Hallock; *A Sonnet,* Pedro J. Saavedra; *The Frown Princess,* Himie Koshevoy; *San Simian,* Gill Krebs; *Run of the Mill,* Cynthia MacGregor;

No Tunes like Show Tunes

A Fairy Funny Story, Cynthia MacGregor; *Art Attack* and *The Son Also Rises,* Bob Dvorak; *A Milestone, Not a Millstone,* James D. Ertner; *Light House Keeping,* Guy Ben-Moshe; *Annie Get Your Pun,* Gary Hallock; *Surreality Show,* Alan B. Combs; *Nobody Doesn't Like Our Show,* Gary Reeves; *An Icicle Built for You,* Gary Hallock;

No Tunes like Show Tunes:
Rodgers and Hammerstein Revue

A Grave Situation, Cynthia MacGregor; *SWAT's It All About?* Bob Dvorak;

Movie Tune News

A New-Fashioned Girl, Ken Pinkham; *The Drunk Backs of Notre Dame* and *A Brand New Name,* Don Hauptman; *Once Pawn a Time,* John W. Price; *On a Roll,* Bob Levi; *Making an Impression,* Gary Hallock; *Tank You,* Bob Dvorak;

Child's Play

The Flea Circuit, Pulling Our Eyes over the Wool, and *Playing to Beat the Band,* Cynthia MacGregor; *True Blue,* Chris Cole; *Egging Them On,* Don Hauptman

Proud to Be an American

The Witching Time of Fright and *Old Soldiers,* Cynthia MacGregor; *Doctor Do-A-Lot*, Glenn Wasson; *Hanky Panky,* Chris Cole; *Jest Ribbon You,* Gary Hallock; *Variety is the Very Spice,* Bob Levi;

That's All Folk

Stepping up to the Plate, Bob Dvorak; *Weed It and Reap,* Lowrie Beachem; *Just for the Halibut,* Sandy Pasquantonio; *Ex Post Fact,* Don Hauptman;

Have a Punny Christmas

Notion for a Lotion, Gary Reeves; *Drama King,* Cynthia MacGregor;

Give Me That Old Time Religion
Scroll Call, Alan B. Combs; *A Finny Tail,* Himie Koshevoy; *Sticky Business,* Gary Hallock; *A Sonnet,* Pedro J. Saavedra;

Go Western, Young Man
The Lone Arranger, Himie Koshevoy; *Bad to Verse,* Alan B. Combs; *Clowning Around,* Sandy Pasquantonio; *Space Opera,* Lin Ka-Ming; *A Sonnet,* Pedro J. Saavedra;

Code of Ethnics
The Server Is Down, Simone van Egeren; *Tilde Cows Come Home* and *Smell Me a River,* Bob Dvorak; *My Little Dumpling,* Bennett Cerf; *Ember Alert,* Susan Blevin; *Leapin' Lizards* and *An In-Tents Adventure,* Cynthia MacGregor;

Songs That Ad Up
Working for Scale and *What a Racket,* Bob Dvorak; *Pulling Our Eyes over the Wool,* Cynthia MacGregor; *A Sonnet,* Pedro J. Saavedra;

Super Agile Punch Lines
Mono a Mono, Bob Levi; *I Have a Little List,* Gil Krebs; *The Bull Whisperer,* Ted Brett;

The Chatty Choo Choo
Talking Point, Paul Dickson; *TV or Not TV,* Ken Shurget; *Light My Fire, Making a Mark, The Wine Ain't Fine"* and *Frosty the No Man,* Jeffrey Sawtelle; *The Two Georges,* Owen K. Lorien; *The Cat/Bird Heat,* Bob Dvorak.

What's Amore?

Various verses by Jim Davis, Jeff Fisher, Alan Freeman, Joseph Hagsmann, Dennis Hammes, Suzie Lemcke, Cynthia MacGregor, Keith Martin, Spider Robinson, Frank Rubin, and Robert Taxon.

Test: A Round of Set-Ups

A Romantic Story, James Charlton; *Par for the Course,* Cynthia MacGregor; *Rings a Bell,* Bennett Cerf; *Gull Meets Buoy,* Alan B. Combs.

Effusive thanks to the members of PUNY for providing original material for this book, especially Cynthia MacGregor, Gary Hallock, Bob Dvorak, and Alan B. Combs.

And much credit is due to Simone van Egeren for tracking down the original lyrics, titles, composers, and lyricists.